Beau ^

THE 22 IMMUTABLE LAWS OF MARKETING IN ASIA

THE 22 IMMUTABLE LAWS OF MARKETING IN ASIA

AL RIES
JACK TROUT
PAUL TEMPORAL

John Wiley & Sons (Asia) Pte Ltd

Originally published in 1993 by HarperBusiness, an imprint of HarperCollins
Publishers, Inc., 10 East 53rd Street, New York, NY 10022, USA

This edition published in 2003 by John Wiley & Sons (Asia) Pte Ltd
2 Clementi Loop, #02-01, Singapore 129809

Published by arrangement with HarperBusiness, an imprint of HarperCollins Publishers,
Inc. New York, New York USA.

This publication is designed to provide accurate and authoritative information in regard to
the subject matter covered. It is sold with the understanding that the publisher is not engaged
in rendering professional services. If professional advice or other expert assistance is
required, the services of a competent professional person should be sought.

Other Wiley Editorial Offices

John Wiley & Sons, Inc., 111 River Street, Hoboken, NJ 07030, USA
John Wiley & Sons Ltd, The Atrium, Southern Gate, Chichester P019, 8SQ, England
John Wiley & Sons (Canada) Ltd, 22 Worcester Road, Rexdale, Ontario M9W 1L1, Canada
John Wiley & Sons Australia Ltd, 33 Park Road (PO Box 1226), Milton, Queensland
4064, Australia
Wiley-VCH, Pappelallee 3, 69469 Weinheim, Germany

Library of Congress Cataloging-in-Publication Data
0-470-82100-0 (paper)

Typeset in 12/18 points, Plantin by Linographic Services Pte Ltd
Printed in Singapore by Saik Wah Press Pte Ltd
10 9 8 7 6 5 4 3 2 1

CONTENTS

Introduction

Asia is now at a crossroads. In most Asian countries, companies have been left far behind as multinational brands have taken their markets by storm, dominating the consumer and, often, the business-to-business categories. OEM (Original Equipment Manufacturing) strategies and weak alliances have been the response, and it is brutal but true to say that it is only in the last few years that many local companies have begun to realize the difference between marketing and sales. And believe us, some still don't.

When Al Ries and Jack Trout wrote *The 22 Immutable Laws of Marketing* in the '90s, they were the first people to state that marketing actually has some laws, and some immutable laws at that!

They opened their book by saying that billions of dollars have been wasted on marketing programs that couldn't possibly work, no matter how clever or brilliant, or how big the budgets. They were not wrong, and unfortunately many companies have not heeded their advice. We still see this in the 21st century despite the warnings they gave, especially in the Asia-Pacific region.

Many managers assume that a well-designed, well-executed, well-financed advertising and promotion program will work. It's not necessarily so, and you don't have to look far in the Asia-Pacific to find this fact, whichever country you happen to be in.

But, we hear you say, the world is different now. Business has changed and so have marketing trends. So do the Immutable Laws of Marketing still apply? Yes, they do, and they are particularly relevant to Asian companies who are fighting inbound competition, driven by deregulation, to make their way in the global marketplace.

In this book you will find the laws have changed only in emphasis to reflect the changing marketplace. And, of course, in the examples chosen to reflect the situation in the Asia-Pacific region.

But there are still 22 laws, and they are still immutable.

1

THE LAW OF LEADERSHIP

It's better to be the first than it is to be better.

The basic issue in marketing is creating a category you can be first in. It's the Law of Leadership: It's better to be first than it is to be better. It's much easier to get into the mind of consumers first than to try to convince people you have a better product than the one that did get there first.

Being first in any category is going to give you the edge. Being second might get you some profits. After that, it's a struggle for survival. Look at Coke and Pepsi. Globally, Coke (the first) outsells Pepsi substantially, but who comes after Pepsi? No one worth bothering about.

Gillette was the first safety razor. Tide was the first laundry detergent. Hewlett-Packard introduced the first desktop laser printer. All are leaders.

How many people have asked for Pampers instead of diapers? This is the success of Procter & Gamble's development of the disposable diaper that revolutionized the diapering habits of consumers worldwide and virtually created the category.

Pampers originated from a P&G researcher who was a grandfather. While caring for his newborn grandchild, he developed a distinct dislike for changing diapers, which perhaps is not really surprising. Research among mothers confirmed that there was a need for something better than cloth diapers. To meet this need, P&G scientists developed a unique three-piece construction to absorb the moisture, distribute it uniformly and transmit fluid to the absorbent core without passing it back to the skin. Additional product innovations have continued to make Pampers a leader and innovator in the category.

P&G's technology in the diaper category has given convenience, comfort and health benefits to parents and children; not to mention huge contributions to P&G's worldwide profits. Pampers is P&G's biggest global brand, generating about US$5 billion or 13% of P&G's US$39 billion in worldwide sales.

Of course, many other players, including Huggies, Drypers, Luvs and Fitti, are now in the marketplace but none has had the success of Pampers worldwide.

It's the same in all walks of life. Talking of which; who was the first man to walk on the moon? Neil Armstrong. Who was the second? You're not so sure. Who was the third? Again, you're not so sure you know, and you probably don't care either.

Yet many companies ignore this rule and wait until a market develops. Then they jump in with a similar or enhanced product, sometimes ignoring another rule (see Chapter 7: The Law of Line Extension). The leading brand in any category is almost always the first brand into the prospect's mind. Coca-Cola in cola. Kellogg's in cereals. IBM in computers. Amazon in Internet book sales. Sun Microsystems in workstations.

Japanese video-game company Nintendo Co. has made its fortune by pioneering not-so-violent games for kids. Super Mario, a character now 21 years old, has US$7 billion in sales around the world. Pokemon seems to be on track for similar results.

In Asia, Colgate has been around for decades, being the first into the market. It has kept abreast of innovations and still maintains a 60–80% market share in some countries. And, however hard the competition tries, it's difficult to dislodge that grip. Heineken was the first imported beer in many foreign markets and still dominates the top end of the beer category in Thailand, for example.

In 1979 something happened that changed the way people listen to music. Market research said it would never work. Retailers were skeptical about sales, and consumers thought that a tape player that could not record would never catch on. So much for market research.

Sony went ahead anyway and introduced the Sony Walkman. The Walkman created a totally new market for portable stereo systems, and, by 1995, over 150 million units had been sold. Lots of other companies have followed, of course, but mention the word "Walkman" and Sony owns the category. Sony has built its business on the relentless pursuit of innovative technology, excellence and quality, driving fashion trends. So successful was the Walkman that it has been praised as one of the three most popular fashion products of the 20th century, together with roller skates and digital watches.

Being first can actually be better than being

better, if you know what we mean. Improvements are always made to product inventions and innovations but the first in has a head start. Naturally, if you are first in to the market and you don't keep ahead then your position will erode over time, but being the leader comes from being first. Sony's Walkman has kept its market leadership by introducing over 300 different models since the launch of the first TPS-L2.

Another reason why the Law of Leadership brings success is that once you are first and get the consumers to buy your brand, often they won't bother to switch. People tend to stick with what they've got. If you meet someone who is apparently a bit better than your wife, husband or partner, most think it's not worth the stress and hassle making the switch, assuming this was possible.

Motorola mobile phones are still holding their own against the mighty Nokia in China because they were first in, not because they have the best products. Carrefour has a commanding share of the hypermarket business because it came in to Asia before the rest, whilst ordinary supermarkets thought they were invincible.

There is another success factor associated with

the Law of Leadership. The first in to the market has the opportunity to have its brand name adopted as the generic category name. So successful is its leadership position that people still use Colgate as the generic name for toothpaste. The first paracetamol-based painkiller product in Asia was Panadol. There are lots of others now, but people stick to Panadol, and again this has become the generic name for the category. Headache? Take some Panadol.

People may buy lots of Canon and other brands of photocopiers but they still want to Xerox their documents (although "zap" is fast replacing that as a word in Singapore). In 1986, the word "Walkman" was included in the Oxford English Dictionary. The founder of Sony, Akio Morita, said that nothing made him happier than the fact that "Walkman" had been accepted around the world as an English word.

So once you are the leader, a position mostly gained by being first, it is pretty hard for competitors to dislodge you, as long as you keep your products up to date and of comparable quality. But if the secret of success is getting into the consumers' minds first, what do most companies do? They pursue the better product strategy. They "benchmark", they employ "total quality management", and they "re-engineer" in the desperate pursuit of operational efficiency and product quality. But marketing is a battle of perceptions not products, as you will see as you read through this book.

∽∾

2

THE LAW OF THE CATEGORY

If you can't be first in a category, change the nature of the category or set up a new category you can be first in.

If you didn't get into the prospect's mind first, don't give up hope. Find a new category you can be first in, or change the nature of the category. There are many ways to be first.

Dell has become the most famous personal computer manufacturer and retailer in Asia by cutting out the middlemen and selling direct to the public. What's more, Dell lets customers order their own tailor-made computers at cheaper prices. What better proposition can consumers get than that? Dell is now attacking the China market and says it is not afraid of the huge low-cost volume producers such as Legend. Legend has a whopping 30% of the China market and its nearest competitor less than 10%. Dell has a little over 4%, but believes its direct-sales model will make a difference which the other players do not have. Dell has started a new category.

Inventing or re-inventing a category is, in many ways, counter to brand-management thinking. Brand managers are often constrained by thinking narrowly rather than broadly. When you have a brand to manage, it's much more likely that you'll be thinking about a) how you can defend its position and brand loyalty, and b) how you can get more consumers to switch from other brands to yours.

Marketing, with its broad approach, allows for a wider view by allowing managers to think "category". When looking at similar brands, prospects tend to have set views and tend to be defensive. People talk about why their brand is better. But when categories change, so do mindsets. They open up to a whole new range of opportunities. Everyone is interested in what's new, but few are interested in what's better.

So the key question when you get a new product to launch is, "What category is it new in?" By creating a "new" category (or the perception of a new category), you become first and it's back to the Law of Leadership again. Two laws in your favor are better than one! Charles Schwab didn't open a better brokerage firm: he opened the first discount brokerage, and then the first Internet brokerage.

One of the most successful companies that has carved out a new product category in flooring is Pergo. The brand is synonymous with laminate flooring. Pergo AB is a Swedish company, but in the U.S., laminate floors are widely referred to as "Pergo" floors. Pergo has achieved household-name status and has generally created consumer confidence in a new flooring product category. Laminates have taken market share from carpet, hardwood, ceramic tile and, primarily, vinyl flooring.

Massage is good for you. It relaxes the muscles and joints, and is de-stressing. Traditionally, body massage is still largely done by expert, well-trained masseurs, but Singapore entrepreneur Dr. Ron Sim saw an opportunity to create a new category in healthcare, which includes massage chairs. The company has been an incredible success even though the products are by no means cheap.

His company — OSIM International — started in 1980 as a retailer of household products, but has established a niche now in developing and marketing healthy-living products to soothe and inspire an individual's mind, body and soul.

OSIM's business is about creating a perspective of the awareness of health. It has established itself as a lifestyle brand that takes a holistic approach to health.

OSIM International aspires to be the global leader in healthy-lifestyle products by enhancing people's quality of life through four focuses — Health Focus, Hygiene Focus, Nutrition Focus and Fitness Focus.

Health Focus is about making the right changes in managing your lifestyle; Hygiene Focus is about clean water, clean air, and a clean environment for homes and offices; Fitness Focus is about bringing the convenience of fitness to the comfort of your home; while Nutrition Focus is about supplementing daily nutritional needs for a balanced diet.

Currently, OSIM has established an extensive distribution network of 320 strategically located stores and counters in Singapore, Hong Kong, Taiwan, China, Malaysia, Indonesia, Thailand, U.S.A., Canada, U.A.E., Australia, U.K., South Africa and Ireland. The intention is to have 1,000 outlets spanning Asia, Europe, the Middle East and the Americas by 2008.

Besides being a leader in quality standards across the world, all OSIM stores carry a consistent holistic approach that places equal emphasis on the mental and physical aspects of health. They have several zones where people can experience different concepts of health and well-being, and come out feeling relaxed and refreshed.

OSIM International is a great example of how, in a crowded healthcare category, there are still opportunities to create new spaces, and successful businesses. It has been rated the #1 brand in Singapore and Hong Kong by the Gallup Organization and AC Nielsen, respectively. And even in the recession year of 2001, group turnover grew 24% and operating profit 25%. These are the rewards that come to category breakers and leaders.

Every newspaper in Asia has its own financial section for those who want local financial news and content. But the coverage is scant. The alternative is to buy international newspapers such as the *Asian Wall Street Journal* and the *Financial Times*, which focus more on non-local issues. So there was no newspaper that catered for readers who wanted some general news and lots of specific financial news — until *The Edge* created that category in

Malaysia. Now it is has entered the Singapore market and is increasing sales all the time.

With travel destinations, the law still applies. People don't go on holiday for shopping, which is available anywhere; they go for other reasons. They will shop, of course, but it is not a prime driver for choosing a holiday.

One of the largest attractions for the leisure traveler is culture. But even the category of holiday destinations is crowded with cultural opportunities; so how does a country appeal to prospective tourists? India can offer Indian culture, China, Chinese culture, and so on. Malaysia is a country with a multicultural population and so it offers a one-stop experience under the banner "Malaysia. Truly Asia" — a new dimension to the category.

What about bread? Well bread is bread is bread, we hear you say. Everywhere there's bread in one form or another — wholemeal, walnut, multigrain, malt, onion, pizza, and even plain old white! The category's full, isn't it? What's new about that? BreadTalk, that's what. There are many types of retailers who sell bread in Asia with all these features and more, and they all looked the same. Then BreadTalk re-invented the category.

Starting with a friendly and memorable name, BreadTalk made buying bread interesting. A first outlet in Singapore, in Bugis Street, in 2000 led to 17 in as many months. Why? The company changed the category by catering for Asian taste buds and, through smart retail design, let customers see the bread being made. Great locations with open access send smells wafting down shopping malls and queues of customers following the smells. The result is customer interest, attraction and interaction, with friendly service to complete the deal.

With a 2001 year-end pre-tax profit of S$2 million on a S$6 million turnover and the prospect of listing, BreadTalk proves you can become a leader through creating a new category. Founder and managing director George Quek used to be in a dead-end job selling dragon candy in 1981, and now he's a category leader.

Maybe you're thinking, "I should have thought of that" or "It's common sense"? Well common sense isn't that common, and there are always opportunities out there to change categories and get customers. BreadTalk has many followers now, but remember the Law of Leadership — they are first in mind and will probably remain market leader.

In fact, to keep its leadership and avoid falling into the fad trap, BreadTalk has an R&D department that introduces new delicious bread products and flavors that replace 20% of the current range every three months. (For more information on fads and trends, see Chapter 18 on The Law of Acceleration.)

You can also change categories across different markets. For instance, D.O.M. (affectionately known as Dirty Old Man in the U.K.) is marketed as a liqueur drink, and a fairly potent one at that. But in Asia it has created another category, as a health and strength restorative for women who have given birth or have been ill.

Jollibee Foods Corporation in the Philippines is pushing out the boundaries in the fast-food category. Not content with ousting McDonald's from #1 in the usual burger section of the category (read more on this in Chapter 4, The Law of Duality), the company has combined local tastes with international efficiency to produce a new chain of fast-food outlets called Chowking.

One thing all Asian countries have in common is that the overseas Chinese have lived in them for generations. The Philippines is no exception, and the ethnic Chinese-Filipinos crave for traditional food, though not in the traditional form. The Philippines has a distinctive American appetite for fast food, and Jollibee's founder, Tony Tan Caktiong, was quick to see the opportunity.

In 2000, he bought the chain of Chinese fast-food restaurants called Chowking, and changed the menus to include wonton soup, dim sum and crispy Chinese noodles, and the environment to his happy, consumer-friendly Jollibee style. The outlets look like burger joints and customers pick what they want, just as they would in a burger place. Speed and value for money, with chopsticks!

Now Chowking has around 200 outlets, sales have increased four-fold since 2000 and the chain is ranked #3, behind Jollibee itself and McDonald's. In his usual entrepreneurial way, Tan is taking the business overseas, with outlets already in California and other countries. But the biggest market of all is on the strategic planning agenda — China itself. Quite a reversal of roles.

But for the most amazing and true example of new category creation try branded bugs. Yes, bugs! People from Thailand have always been regarded as having great creativity but this beats the lot.

In some parts of Asia, Thailand being one, insects have traditionally been part of the poorer people's diet. They have traditionally been in the snack category. But now they are the latest fast-food success for the middle classes. Insects Inter has around 60 franchises selling crickets, grasshoppers, coconut worms, scorpions, water beetles and other things that crawl and make most of us feel ill.

The company hopes to have 200 outlets by the end of 2003, and is going into the canned-bug business. Nicely boxed and branded, and sold by sales people wearing yellow shirts and baseball caps with a coconut worm logo, these pesticide-free bugs are aimed at modern young adults — the new generation. To catch the more upscale crowd, there are even outlets in foreign hypermarkets such as Tesco Lotus and Carrefour. McDonald's might have to move aside for McCrawlies!

Now Insect Inter has leadership and is first in mind when it comes to packaged bugs, and, yes, they are selling well.

3

THE LAW OF THE LADDER

The strategy to use depends on which rung you occupy on the ladder.

Whilst being first into the prospect's mind ought to be your primary marketing objective, the battle isn't lost if you fail in this endeavor. There are strategies to use for the #2 and #3 brands.

All products are not created equal. There's a hierarchy in the mind that prospects use in making decisions.

For each category, there is a product ladder in the mind. On each rung there is a brand name. Your marketing strategy should depend on how soon you got into the mind and consequently which rung of the ladder you occupy. Higher is better, of course. In Asia's category for batteries, the positions change depending on the country, but the top three in the category are always Duracell, Energizer and Panasonic.

In the local Singapore banking sector, the trio is UOB, DBS and OCBC. They have the volume but are under pressure from the foreign banks. In the not-too-distant future, the trio will become a duo (see Chapter 4, The Law of Duality).

In the Asian logistics market, FedEx, DHL and TNT dominate.

In the new and fast-growing retail business in China, the ladder is rapidly forming. China's retail market is worth about US$450 billion and growing at 10% per year. In the four biggest cities — Beijing, Shanghai, Guangzhou and Chengdu — the modern retail trade, characterized by hypermarkets, supermarkets, department and convenience stores, already accounts for around 60% of sales.

The foreign players are diving into China to take advantage of this. French retailer Carrefour is in the lead with 31 stores; Wal-Mart is second with 22; PriceSmart has 21; and these are followed by Metro with 15, and Makro with seven. Some of them are talking about doubling their numbers in the next year or two. Now they are established, they will take some beating, and the leading home-grown supermarket chain, Lianhua, is having to restructure in the face of competition.

The mind is selective. Prospects use their ladders in deciding which information to accept and which to reject. In general, a mind accepts only new data that is consistent with its product ladder in that category. Everything else is ignored.

What about your product's ladder in the prospect's mind? How many rungs are there on your ladder? It depends on whether your product is a high-interest or low-interest product. Products you use every day (toothpaste, skincare, shampoo, fresh milk) tend to be high-interest products with many rungs on their ladders. Products that are bought infrequently (furniture, luggage) usually have few rungs on their ladders.

Products that involve a great deal of pride, prestige and status (watches, cars) are also high-interest products, even though they are purchased infrequently. But if you focus on prestige cars, then the choice comes down to Mercedes, BMW and depending on which Asian country you are in, Rolls Royce, Lexus or Jaguar.

Products that are purchased infrequently and involve an unpleasant experience usually have few rungs on their ladders. Car batteries and tires, and life insurance are examples of these.

There is a relationship between market share and your position on the ladder in the prospect's mind. You tend to have twice the market share of the brand below you and half the market share of the brand above you.

Marketing people often talk about the "three leading brands" in a category as if it were a battle of equals. It almost never is. The leader inevitably dominates the #2 brand which, in turn, inevitably smothers #3. Take the beer market in Malaysia. In the non-premium category, Carlsberg dominates both Tiger and Anchor, which was once the leader.

What's the maximum number of rungs on a ladder? There seems to be a rule of seven in the minds of prospects. Ask people to name all the brands they can remember in a given category, and rarely will anyone name more than seven. And that's for a high-interest category. So, for laptop/notebook computers in Asia, people will remember IBM, Toshiba, Sony, Dell, Acer, Fujitsu and Twinhead.

The US$3.5-billion bottled-water market has literally hundreds of different brands in the category. However, slowly but surely the market is in the process of being dominated by three brands: Aquafina, (bottled by Pepsi-Cola), Dasani (bottled by Coca-Cola) and Poland Spring. In the long run, we expect these three brands to dominate the market.

Sometimes your own ladder, or category, is too small. It might be better to be a small fish in a big pond than to be a big fish in a small pond. In other words, it's sometimes better to be #3 on a big ladder than #1 on a small ladder.

The ladder is a simple, but powerful, analogy that can help you deal with the critical issues in marketing. Before starting any marketing program, ask yourself the following questions: Where are we on the ladder in the prospect's mind? On the top rung? On the second rung? Are we on the ladder at all?

Then make sure your program deals realistically with your position on the ladder. We will discuss more on how to do this later.

4

THE LAW OF DUALITY

In the long run, every market becomes a two-horse race.

Early on, a category is a ladder of many rungs. Gradually, the ladder becomes a two-rung affair.

In burgers, it's McDonald's and Burger King, except in the Philippines where it is Jollibee and McDonald's, a success story we'll tell you about in a moment.

In photographic film, it's Kodak and Fuji. In Asia's skies, it's Singapore Airlines and Cathay Pacific. In aircraft, its Boeing and Airbus. In payment cards, it's Visa and Mastercard. In computer printers, it's Canon and HP. Nintendo and Sony dominate the computer game market. In the long run, marketing is a two-horse race.

When you take the long view in marketing, you find the battle usually winds up as a titanic struggle between two major players — usually the old reliable brand and the upstart.

Jollibee is the upstart that beat the reliable brand, McDonald's, in the Philippines — a feat we have not heard of elsewhere in the world in the burger fast-food category. Jollibee started as an ice-cream parlor in 1975, but the founder, Tony Tan Caktiong, saw fast-food chains like McDonald's, Burger King and Wendy's taking off in a big way and wanted to join the race.

Filipinos like foreign brands but, instead of joining up with one of them, Tan decided to go it alone with Filipino taste products, such as moist hamburgers, crispy fried chicken and a noodle dish called *pansit palabok* and other products. Today, it has 200 outlets and its turnover of around US$230 million is double that of McDonald's. Jollibee is now going into other Asian countries and, believe or not, the U.S.

The law even applies with destinations. In India, which has one of the world's most talented IT workforces, the race is on between two cities to become India's Silicon Valley. Bangalore had the leadership position for the last few years, but upstart Hyderabad is challenging hard. Both cities are building international airports and are crazy about technology. In Bangalore, software tycoons enjoy the cult status of the "Bollywood" film stars and the nation's cricketers. In Hyderabad, food outlets like y2chicken@tandoori.com are in vogue. Bangalore is still the king, but the upstart #2 is catching up fast.

Are these results pre-ordained? Of course not. In developing markets, such as those in Asia, deregulation and the liberalization of markets can suddenly create massive opportunities. In Taiwan, Taiwan Beer claims that it's the leading beer and that it's clearly ahead of the competition. This is, of course, a legitimate claim as until recently it's been the only beer you could buy. For more than a century, it had been the only one because it was a government monopoly — Taiwan's "official" beer, created and managed by what used to be known as the Taiwan Government's Tobacco & Wine Monopoly Bureau.

Although the beer market has been opened up to foreign players for several years now, distribution and price advantages have kept competition to a minimum. Heineken, Miller, Beck's and Kirin had tried unsuccessfully to buy their way in with big advertising spend. Only recently, when Taiwan joined the WTO, have things begun to change.

The best-selling beer in China, Tsingtao, has entered in a big way, claiming 30,000 outlets and 5% market share after only three months. Imported by Tsing Beer Corporation (TBC) in a joint venture with Taiwan's Sanyo Whishbih Group, Tsingtao, TBC confidently predicts, will have 30% within three years. And instead of positioning itself as an imported beer, it has taken the incumbent head on, including trying (and, by most accounts, succeeding) to de-throne Taiwan Beer's ownership of "freshness". Taiwan has always been a tough market but Tsingtao has the potential to be a global brand. So what was virtually a monopoly market is almost certainly going to be a duopoly.

Watch out for Tsingtao as a formidable regional Asian, if not global, brand. It has great ambitions. In the United States it is the best-selling Chinese beer, with distribution primarily through Chinese restaurants, which are very popular in America.

Changing market fundamentals and legislation can give rise to opportunities in marketing, but there are other laws of marketing that can also affect the results. Furthermore, your marketing programs can strongly influence your sales, providing they are in tune with the laws of marketing. When you're a weak #3, you're not going to make much progress by going out and attacking the two strong leaders. What you can do is carve out a profitable niche for yourself (see Chapter 6, The Law of Focus).

Knowing that marketing is a two-horse race in the long run can help you plan strategy in the short run.

There is a very interesting battle going on in the video-games market. So far, it's been a two-horse race between platform makers Nintendo and Sony. In games used on the platforms, Nintendo has won the battle for the kids' market, with characters like Pokemon and Super Mario. But even though it has sold over 100 million units and expects to sell more than 12 million in 2002, Nintendo is now restricted as more and more mature segments join the games market. Sony has a better share of the teens and 20+ market, with more aggressive and violent games.

But Sony has an overall 75% share of the console market worldwide with its PlayStations, whilst Nintendo's GameCube console is second.

But there are two newcomers that have joined the race — Microsoft with its Xbox, and Nokia with its N-Gage.

The games played determine the console or platform market, and consequently there is a huge scramble now to secure the best games that will attract the widest market. All four combatants are spending massive budgets leading up to the end-of-year holiday season. For example, by Christmas 2002 Nintendo is likely to have around 180 games, and Microsoft more than 200. Sony is expected to outdo them both, with more than 350. Nokia is just entering the arena but cannot be underestimated. Its brand power, marketing know-how and wireless expertise may well dislodge the others. Not in the short term, but it will certainly change the nature of the category in the long term.

Nintendo is now not just fighting for overall market share against Sony; it's fighting for survival. So someone is going to become #3 and #4 in the not-so long run. We envision a massive marketing battle but, looking ahead, the Law of Duality and the Law of the Ladder will eventually prevail. As we write, in the U.S., Microsoft's Xbox has already become the second-most popular video-game player, behind Sony's PlayStation. This puts a lot of pressure on the third brand, Nintendo's GameCube. We expect that the GameCube will slowly fade away.

Successful marketers concentrate on the two top rungs. Jack Welch, the legendary ex-chairman and CEO of General Electric, once said: "Only businesses that were #1 or #2 in their markets could win in the increasingly competitive global arena. Those that could not were fixed, closed or sold."

It's this kind of thinking that built companies like Unilever. Unilever is now in the process of reducing the number of its brands from 1,600 to 400. It's concentrating on its power brands — the ones that already are or can be either #1 or #2 in their chosen markets.

Early on, in a developing market, the #3 or #4 positions look attractive. Sales are increasing. New, relatively unsophisticated customers are coming into the market. These customers don't always know which brands are the leaders, so they pick ones that look interesting or attractive. Quite often, these turn out to be the #3 or #4 brands.

As time goes on, however, these customers get educated. They want the leading brand, based on the somewhat naïve assumption that the leading brand must be better.

We repeat: The customer believes that marketing is a battle of products. It's this kind of thinking that keeps the two brands on the top: "They must be the best; they're the leaders."

5

THE LAW OF THE MIND AND PERCEPTION

Marketing is not a battle of products, it's a battle of perceptions; and sometimes it's better to be first in the mind than to be first in the marketplace.

There is nothing wrong with the Law of Leadership — it works. But, over time, perceptions can change and you can get to be first in the mind, which is everything in marketing. The real importance of being first in the mind lies in occupying #1 position in the mind. IBM was not the first computer into the marketplace but won the battle early on with substantial marketing effort.

If there is one law that every marketing person needs to know about, it's this one. Marketing is a battle of perception not product, and so the mind takes preference over the marketplace. But as many would-be entrepreneurs and companies have found out to their cost, great ideas are one thing; getting them into the minds of others is another. And once a mind is made up, then it is difficult to change it.

Xerox tried for many years to move into the computer business after being first in copiers, but got nowhere and spent billions in the process.

Thailand is a great destination, offering tourists everything they could possibly want. But, despite many costly attempts to change people's minds, it is still heavily associated with the sex industry.

Tiger Balm has positive perceptions. It is a herbal ointment positioned as an Asian product that originated in the Imperial courts of China, whose warlords and emperors needed relief from aches, pains and a variety of other ailments. It has a tremendous following in Asia amongst all age groups, and consumers believe it is the answer to various heath problems. It now sells in more than 70 countries.

Why did Toyota have to create the Lexus to get into the luxury car market? Because people would not believe that Toyota could produce a luxury car.

China and other Asian countries suffer from a product-quality perception problem. If it's

"Made in China", it can't be good. One day, the head of Haier — the white-goods manufacturer — took his staff into the factory yard, where they saw defective products they had produced. He took a sledgehammer to every one of the products to demonstrate the need for quality to his staff. Haier produces world-class quality, but would we believe it if it came with the "Made in China" tag? Probably not. That's why Haier now has a factory in the U.S., producing high-class goods with a "Made in U.S.A." tag.

Sometimes having a strong position in consumers' minds can work for you in a very positive way, and sometimes in a negative way. Volvo is famous for its mind-grip regarding safety; a brand image strength it has enjoyed for many decades. Today, if you walk down the street in Asia and ask people what is the safest car, back will come the answer "Volvo", even though many other cars are now just as safe.

This has worked well for Volvo for many years and the message is still being reinforced. In October 2002, Volvo announced an in-vehicle safety-communications system called Volvo On Call Plus, which notifies you if you are in a crash (in case you hadn't realized), and offers other services. These include "Mayday", which automatically calls for help and determines the severity of the crash, even if airbags don't deploy. Volvo will continue its innovations in the world of driving safety, because it owns the word in car driving.

Is there a problem for Volvo? Well there is, because it wants to get away from the other aspect related to safety in consumers' minds. Safety has become so entwined in people's minds with the heavy, tank-like models that Volvo used to produce, that they now don't believe that the brand can produce sporty high-performance cars. And most drivers want power on the roads. As a consequence, Volvo has spent millions of dollars in recent years on rallying, advertising and design in an attempt to change this image. It's still spending. Several years ago it introduced the S70 line of sports cars, including an S70 convertible. Needless to say, the cars sold poorly. Once perceptions are established, people's minds don't change fast. So, in 2002, Volvo revealed its new future safety concept car, showing what the best safety attributes of future cars are likely to be. So despite efforts to sell new design vehicles like the S and XC series, they keep having to go back to their safety image.

Many companies think that having the best product, in whatever way, will win the marketing battle. This is why there is a preoccupation with market research that gathers all the facts about features, attributes and other product aspects. Armed with this knowledge, they march confidently into the marketplace convinced that they have the best product and that this will bring success.

They are so often wrong. The reason why there are winners in markets is not because of product superiority. After all, when competitors can copy your products, services, technology, systems and just about everything else, where is the advantage? Volvo may be matched in safety features by other brands. Attributes and figures do not make winners; perceptions do. It's what people think that counts, not what researchers say. Often in market research, people do not say what they really think and feel, despite the apparent openness. Only by studying how perceptions are formed in the mind and focusing your marketing programs on them can you overcome incorrect marketing instincts.

It is easy to see the power of perception over product. Take taste in soft drinks, for example.

The Coca-Cola Company conducted 200,000 taste tests that "proved" that New Coke tasted better than Pepsi-Cola but that Pepsi tasted better than their original formula they called Coca-Cola Classic. But who won the marketing battle? Not the drink that proved to be the best taste — New Coke; that came in third. The one that research showed tasted the worst is still in first place. The original Coca-Cola has remained ahead of all other cola drinks. New Coke went nowhere.

You believe what you want to believe. You taste what you want to taste. Soft-drink marketing is a battle of perceptions, not a battle of taste.

All truth is relative; relative to your mind or the mind of someone else. Whether you think you are right and someone else is wrong is really you saying that you perceive the situation more accurately than the other person. But marketing managers and directors all too often focus on the facts they can find because they are trained to believe in objective reality. They're also easier to justify to boards of directors! If they think that a better product is needed to win a marketing battle then it becomes easier to believe they have the best product. In other words, they make the facts fit their own perceptions.

The reality is, however, that it is what people out there in the marketplace looking to buy products perceive to be true that is the truth. Perception can be fact or fiction, but what exists in the thoughts of each individual is reality to him or her. In the case of Classic Coke, it was people's perception that it was "the real thing" that was uppermost in their minds. Therefore, everything else in perception terms was a copy and not authentic, regardless of taste.

The task of marketers is to establish or change consumer perceptions, because if they don't they will not win the battle. Will Shell ever convince us that it is more interested in saving the planet's resources rather than using them up? It's spending millions of dollars to try and change our perceptions, and is going to have to go on spending for a long time.

Minds are powerful things, and changing people's minds is a difficult task. Whenever anyone is introduced in any way to anything for any length of time they immediately form a view of it in their mind — a perception. Perceptions are automatic — the mind forms them whether we like them and want them or not; they play an important role. in our everyday lives and the decisions we make. Positive perceptions lead to positive actions and vice versa.

The mind is much more adept at storing and retrieving data than the best of today's supercomputers, and it can store up millions (or even billions) of perceptions, allocating them to various "positions" in the brain, like a huge filing cabinet. So positions are like files, and good perceptions are good filing spots at the front of people's minds. You do not have to be first into the market to do this; but how you position your brands is important.

Keep reading, because the other laws will help you with your management of people's perceptions.

6

THE LAW OF FOCUS

The most powerful concept in marketing is
owning a word in the prospect's mind.

A company can become incredibly successful if it can find a way to own a word in the mind of the prospect. Not a complicated word — a simple one. This is the Law of Focus. You "burn" your way into the mind by narrowing the focus to a single word or concept.

In a way, the Law of Leadership — it's better to be first than to be better — enables the first brand or company to own a word in the mind of consumers. But the word the leader owns is often so simple that it's invisible.

The leader owns the word that stands for the category. For many years, IBM owned "computer". Coca-Cola owns "cola"; "luggage" is owned by Samsonite; think "big bikes", think Harley-Davidson. Volvo owns "safety". It's the word-association test you can play with your friends, and it is a test for the validity of a leadership claim. Think "vodka" think Absolut. In Asia, when people think of "insect bites" they think of Mopiko; for "medical oil", Axe brand; for "things that hurt" it's Tiger Balm.

The thing that astute leaders know is that you can't take a competitor's word. It's back to the mind again; once a prospect's mind is made up, it's difficult to change it. The concept of Windows as the computer operating system will never be taken by anyone else. Microsoft will remain permanently associated with this concept and word. Similarly, Intel owns the concept of the computer chip.

When people think about buying oyster sauce they think Lee Kum Kee. It has instant word association for those people who cook Chinese food. This Hong Kong company started up in 1888 and is still privately owned. Sticking to its basic cooking-sauce-and-condiment category, Lee Kum Kee has now developed a product range that sells on five continents, with annual sales around US$100 million.

Founded in 1870, Eu Yan Sang is another company with a strong heritage and focuses still on traditional Chinese medicines and herbs. It has, however, made sure that it remains relevant to modern and new target audiences by adapting its products by way of taste, flavor and sales channels. Chief executive Richard Eu has created a brand and marketing strategy that gives Asian and non-Asian consumers the best of tradition and modernity.

One of the great successes in the hospitality category is Banyan Tree Hotels and Resorts. In a crowded market place, and when economies suffer from volatility and recessions, making money in the luxury end of the market is difficult to sustain. But Banyan Tree has done it. Why? Because it focused on its niche part of the category offering "romance and intimacy". Everything appeals to people who want to share those kinds of moments. Products are in line with customers' expectations, offering "Sanctuary for the Senses". Health packages with names like Sea of Senses, Oasis of Harmony and Voyage of Peace are irresistible. It even offers underwater weddings in its Maldives outlet.

Banyan Tree management has guarded its focus and brand well, turning down many offers of joint-venture activities that do not fit the values and service quality. The company as a result is going from strength to strength. Focus like this makes it hard for competitors to break in and sustain high profitability.

The essence of marketing is narrowing the focus. You become stronger when you reduce the scope of your operations. You can't stand for something if you chase after everything. Too many companies fail because, having established a niche, they get overconfident and less focused on what they are good at. Mega-mergers and acquisitions occur in big business all the time only to be followed at some later date by spin-offs, sell-offs and a return to core competencies.

Success can go to companies' heads too. British Airways went into many travel-related businesses but didn't make the cut. People think of it as an airline. Singapore Airlines concentrates on air travel service and owns the concept.

Intel owns computer chips, but it is becoming edgy about so much focus and lack of growth in chip markets and has started to move into manufacturing components for toys, and consumer devices such as portable digital music players.

Royal Selangor is famous for its pewter products to the point where it owns the word "pewter" in Asia. It has created a global brand in a very niche market, but its forays into the more competitive worlds of jewelry, gold and silver brands have yet to pay off. Whilst pewter and the others are all metal-based products, pewter is not a cashable item, and this makes a difference.

There are some words that are difficult to own but still companies chase after them. Take "quality", for instance. So many companies lay claim to this word, but who wouldn't? No company wants to go around saying it isn't producing top-quality goods or services. In fact, quality is no longer a different-iator in the world of marketing; it is a prerequisite. You cannot build a powerful brand without it.

Some companies accept the need to focus and own words or concepts but try to accomplish this strategy in ways that are self-defeating. So Ford's "Quality is Job 1" slogan did nothing to change people's perceptions about Ford. Indeed, the fact that they had to mention it at all might have made people wonder why.

If you're really going to lay claim to quality then potential customers won't believe you unless you focus on high-priced products only, as BMW does. It cleverly sidesteps the quality issue by saying it is "The Ultimate Driving Machine". So top quality is implied but not directly mentioned. No one else can claim those words, but BMW has to live up to them with everything it produces and does. Losing out to Ferrari in the 2002 Formula 1 series by massive distances, points and reliability did not help reinforce the message and people's perceptions.

The media continues to report mega-mergers that haven't worked and are now being dismantled as businesses that have no relationship to each other become mismanaged. The message is this. If you want to focus — and you should — focus on something that is not just different from the rest, but something you can continue to deliver better than anyone else. And continue delivering it! Don't get sidetracked into growth by category extensions and businesses you do not belong in.

❧❧

7

THE LAW OF EXTENSION

There's an irresistible pressure to extend the equity of the brand.

This is the biggest trap companies can fall into. It is the most violated law in the book. What's even more dangerous about line extension is that it tends to occur continuously, often with almost no conscious effort on the part of the company.

But first let's clarify what we mean. A company can embark on line extensions and brand extensions. A line extension means using the brand name of a successful product to offer a new product or service in the same category. Toyota has the Corolla and the Camry, for instance. A brand extension involves the use of an existing brand name to move into a new product or service category. Ford Motor Company has started a Jaguar bank, for example.

When we talk about extensions in this book, we are referring to both, because both can be just as appealing and equally dangerous. When a company or one of its products becomes successful, hearts tend to overrule heads in boardrooms. Success plants the seeds for future problems. The issue really is that the further you are tempted to move away from the positioning strength of your brand in consumers' minds, the less successful you are likely to be.

Intel has made billions through being the world's #1 manufacturer of semiconductors, but has now made a strategic decision to manufacture other products such as ChatPad, an instant messaging and e-mail device, and WebTablet, which allows people to surf the Net using a hardcover-book-sized wireless screen. The company is also going into devices that connect to and increase the value of home computers. However, by getting into different categories it is going to encounter different competitors, such as Sony, Philips and Rio. Then life may not be so good.

The extension temptation is always there. Take Virgin, Sir Richard Branson's group of companies, for example. His Virgin music label was his first great success. Then he branched out into other industries (eventually selling the Virgin music brand)

and now has over 200 businesses under the umbrella brand. Some have been successful. For example, he took on British Airways in the courts and made his own airline Virgin Atlantic a success. Now Virgin Atlantic has a joint venture with Singapore Airlines, for which Sir Richard received a great deal of money. What Singapore Airlines has gained is not so clear. The Virgin brand name adds little to that of one of the finest airlines in the world, nor does it give Singapore Airlines global reach, and the service cultures are very different.

Not all the Virgin extensions have gone so smoothly. Virgin Vodka has all but disappeared, and Virgin Cosmetics is not a money-spinner at all. Virgin Cola has not done well either. Worse still, in Asia, a S$1-billion joint venture (Virgin Mobile) with Singapore Telecoms, started in 2001, has had to close down in 2002 because of a chronic lack of subscribers. You cannot have a successful brand extension if you don't understand the market.

When you try to be all things to all people, you inevitably wind up in trouble. It's better to be strong in one area than weak in many. There are as many ways to extend your brand as there are galaxies in the universe, and new ways are invented every day. In the long run, and in the presence of serious competition, line extensions almost never work.

Wherever you look there are brand extensions, which is one reason why stores are choked with brands. But in spite of the fact that extensions often don't work, companies continue to pump them out. Here are some examples:

- Calvin Klein: Calvin Klein cologne/perfume
- Mercedes-Benz: Mercedes-Benz watches
- Caterpillar: Cat apparel
- Wrigley: Pharmaceutical gums

Coca-Cola, still the world's most valuable brand (just), has decided to add another line extension via the flavor Vanilla Coke. After the New Coke disaster, and the Cherry Coke sales, you'd think that the company would have learnt an important lesson about extensions. It is in grave danger of diluting its core brand, and causing confusion and disappointment among consumers.

Apart from market research, which sometimes gives you the wrong answers anyway, simple common sense tells you what could be a winner and what could be a loser. But sometimes common sense is not very common. The further you move away from your core business and brand positioning, the greater your chances of failure.

Some companies resist the temptation though, and we ought to give them some credit. Rolex realized the need to reach a wider target audience but also knew that producing a middle-market watch would damage the prestige Rolex image. So it launched Tudor.

Realizing that to extend to the youth and other markets its brand name just wouldn't fit the bill, Casio created G-Shock and Baby-G. Toyota knew that to reach up into the luxury, prestige-car market with its brand would be a disaster, so it launched Lexus. Nissan is doing a similar thing with Infiniti. The first three of these examples have been successful by avoiding the extension trap. The fourth remains to be seen.

By contrast, Mercedes-Benz has gone down-market with the "A" series, a move acknowledged privately as a mistake, and Porsche has extended its brand into the sports-utility-vehicle category. Porsche will face damage to its image and its profits in years to come, just as Mercedes is doing now.

In the conventional view, a business strategy usually consists of developing an all-encompassing vision. In other words, what concept or idea is big enough to hold all of a company's current products and services as well as those that are planned for the future?

In the conventional view, strategy is a tent. You put up a tent big enough to hold everything you might possibly want to get into it. But the size of the tent you put up is an inside-out decision. Other companies have other tents, and consumers might think your tent is not so weatherproof. So you might end up in the tent without the people you want to be with.

The modern view is that brands now drive corporate strategy. In fact, brand visions are now replacing corporate visions, so powerful is their impact on profits. But brands cannot be abused. Think of it as how a doctor would approach a medical transplant. There has got to be a thorough diagnosis of the patient and a good match found with the brand. Any brand extension must match the patient; otherwise rejection will occur.

- *More is less.* The more products, the more markets, the more alliances a company makes, the less money it makes. "Full-speed in all directions" seems to be the call from the corporate bridge. When will companies learn that many brand and line extensions ultimately lead to failure?

- *Less is more.* If you want to be successful today, you have to narrow the focus in order to build a position in the prospect's mind. If you have a strong position, then extensions based on what consumers really value in your brand might work.

For many companies, an extension is the easy way out. Launching a brand requires not only money, but also an idea or concept. For a new brand to succeed, it ought to be the first in a new category (see Chapter 1, The Law of Leadership). Or the new brand ought to be positioned as an alternative to the leader (see Chapter 20, The Law of the Opposite). Companies that wait until a new market has developed often find these two leadership positions already occupied. So they fall back on the old reliable line-extension approach.

Companies must realize that brands only extend or stretch as much as consumers will allow them to. In the absence of concrete research that tells you unequivocally that the extension will be accepted, don't fall into the trap. The antidote for impulsive brand extension is corporate courage, a commodity in short supply.

≈≈

8

THE LAW OF EXCLUSIVITY AND SUPERIORITY

Owning a superior position in the consumer's mind is vital; marketing is a continuous search for exclusivity.

This Law concentrates on not just owning a word in the prospect's mind, but owning words, relationships and self-expression in the prospect's mind, particularly in relation to prestige and status.

Buying and owning powerful luxury brands helps inform the world of your wealth. These brands can also be used to express what people think, love, admire, aspire to become, and many other psychological motivators. They express a person's personality and the people they like to be with, and sometimes the brand manufacturers (such as Harley-Davidson) build brand personalities to suit their target audiences. The Body Shop has been very successful in Asia through its unique ownership of environmental and social issues.

In Asia, prestige is king. *Kia Su* reigns. The exact meaning conveyed by this phrase is that people do not want to be losers. They are very competitive and want to win. So you buy something, and then you want something more and/or better. Your friends get something and you want to go one step further. You want to be one step ahead. Condominiums, cars, careers, credit cards and other items all serve as demonstrations of the *Kia Su* syndrome

On initiating a conversation with an Asian person, questions tend to revolve around issues like "Where do you come from? Where do you live? What do you drive? Where is your office?, "Which floor?" and so on. There is nothing wrong with this. It denotes a natural curiosity and sense of ambition that is derived from a history of suffering and development. Asian people work harder and smarter than many of their Western counterparts. Desire and wealth are a part of the Asian culture because of past deprivation and colonialism. But what is important in marketing is that the mindset of success is alive and well

As a consequence, luxury brands do well in Asia. Hermes has sold more scarves in this last recession than ever before. And Armani sold more during this last recession than before the recession set in. It's actually not purely an Asian phenomenon, but a universal psychological need — people want to express themselves through brands.

For instance, most people don't carry around bags of money to express their wealth (well, sometimes they do and they get caught out entering different countries) but they do buy, wear and use brands that demonstrate their wealth. A person wanting to portray that they have "made it" in Asia will pay one thousand times the price of a Casio watch to wear a Rolex watch. Rolex is a symbol of "arrival". Status and prestige are so important in Asia.

In Hong Kong, hotels usually arrange transport from the airport for their guests. The better the hotel, the better the transport. Needless to say, the top hotels such as The Peninsula are always recording high occupancy rates, and you will find yourself riding into town in a Rolls Royce. In Asia, if you want to impress, price is not a consideration. People express their wealth through tangible products and services — the best, most exclusive brands.

Another company that owns the self-expression

of success is Mercedes. When you can afford a Mercedes, you've arrived. Before the last recession, when the price of Mercedes cars went up in Malaysia, the waiting list got longer each time. Sales people for Mercedes were so confident and complacent that they would not go out and see customers; customers had to go to them! Getting a test drive was a major achievement.

You can hardly go to a meeting now in any boardroom without spotting a Mont Blanc pen (sorry, "writing instrument") poking out of some executive's pocket!

Exclusivity rules amongst the rich and famous. In Malaysia, for example, Christian Dior evidently has three clients who spend over US$5 million on dresses annually. Worldwide, Christian Dior has 2,000 people that fall into this spending category. Each dress is usually worn only once.

In the luxury categories it is possible for many brands to lay claim to the words "exclusivity", "prestige" and "status". Outside the luxury category, it is difficult to own a word that a competitor owns. However, there are some examples.

As we have seen in Asia and throughout the world, Volvo owns "safety" and no other manufacturer has the same credibility in that area. In motorcycles, it is Honda that has by far the greatest market share in nearly all Asian countries. Suzuki is a long way behind and determined to catch up, but Honda owns the word at present.

Education and qualifications are also highly prized on Asia, at whatever level. If you really want to make it in *Kia Su* education, the local universities aren't good enough — it's got to be Harvard or Oxbridge. When going for jobs, candidates appear with stacks of paperwork to demonstrate what they have learnt and succeeded in achieving. IT is the future, so we are told, and technology is increasingly becoming part of our everyday lives. In Asia, children are learning computer skills at a very early age.

Informatics saw what was coming a long time ago and owns technology (IT) training in Asia. Established in 1983, it is now challenging leading brands in business education also. It has several brands including Purple Train, I-skills Alliance and Thames Business School. From modest beginnings in Singapore, it now has over 450 education and training centers in 42 countries.

The Law of Exclusivity and Superiority has special significance in Asia. If you can establish a niche in a category related to these words, you will have a good business. Would you prefer to travel from Singapore to Bangkok on an ordinary train or on the Orient Express? Mmm!

9

THE LAW OF DIVISION

Over time, a category will divide and become two or more categories.

The marketing arena is an ever-expanding ocean of categories.

A category starts off as a single entity but, over time, it breaks up into sub-segments. The computer category is a good example. Once upon a time there were computers. Now there are super-computers, mainframes, workstations, desktops, laptops, notebooks, palm tops and pen computers. The latest item to spread panic and buying confusion among us is the Tablet PC. Claimed to be "The next PC revolution", Acer from Taiwan has announced its tablet computer, developed "in close collaboration with Microsoft Corporation". To further add to our insatiable appetite for innovation and confusion, the flier text reads: "Featuring a unique convertible design offering standard notebook and Tablet PC modes, the wireless and ultra-portable TravelMate C100 is the take-anywhere computer everyone's been waiting for." Well, that's clear enough isn't it?

The further categories divide, the more consumers tend to get confused.

Another example is the unbelievable combinations of computer chips and other options that can be packaged up for the consumer. For example, Intel — which at one time claimed its brand shorthand made decisions easier for all of us with Pentium — now confuses us with Pentium 1, 2,3,4, Celeron, Xeon, and so on! And word has it Pentium 5 is on the way to add more confusion. And that's only from one company!

Once there was a car. Now we see luxury cars, medium-priced cars and inexpensive cars. There are stretch cars, long-wheelbase, intermediates, compacts, compact sport utility, and compact tall-wagons. There are sports cars, sports-utility vehicles, four-wheel drives, all-wheel drives, coupes, hatchbacks, pickups, wagons, cross-country wagons, and the list goes on.

Things are getting very mixed up. Carlos Ghosn, CEO of Nissan Motor Co. and widely acknowledged as the "guru" of automobile business turnaround and development, has said, astutely: "I think you're going to see an explosion in crossovers."

This could have two meanings. The first meaning, which we have all gleaned from the above, is that everything is crossing over into different parts of other parts of the whole category. The second meaning, and the one that Ghosn was referring to apparently, is that there is another division of the segment now — the crossover vehicle, of which Subaru is the acknowledged pioneer. A crossover is a vehicle that combines off-road capability (in case you go off the road?), durability (for those who treat their cars really badly?), the easy handling of a car (so we know it's not an actual car?), with the space of a sports-utility vehicle (in which you can go to, and play, many sports?). How divisive can division be?

Wine sales are rising all the time in Asia. Wine is really getting popular amongst all age groups, giving rise to many opportunities, and the category is growing just as rapidly. It used to be easy ordering wines; red or white — period. But today the art of wine drinking has changed dramatically and being *au fait* with the etiquette of wine is considered one-upmanship. Now we have red wines, white wines, dessert wines, sparkling wines and ice wines! In addition to this, wines are further divided into categories such as Shiraz, Rosé, Grenache, Zinfandel, Pinot Noir, Merlot, Cabernet Sauvignon, Chardonnay, Sauvignon Blanc, Riesling, etc, depending on the dominant grape from which they're made.

To add to the confusion, there is also appellation, which is not always there on labeling. This is usually defined by laws in the country in which the wine was made and quite often represents a sub-region where the wine was made (Margaux, Bordeaux, Saint-Emilion Grand Cru, etc). So wine owners have many ways to market their brands and this has made life so much more interesting for the true-blue "wine connoisseurs". Unfortunately, if you're not an expert and just want a decent glass of wine, things can get really confusing.

With beer, too, life has become more complicated. We are confronted with several hundred brands in a category that is now separated out into foreign, national, premium, mid-priced and low-range, lite, draft, lagers, ales, stouts, pilseners, darks, and more.

The point we want to make here is that categories will always divide, because markets are always fragmenting, as more and more consumers want more and customization. Each segment is a separate, distinct category. Each segment has its own reason for existence. And each segment has its own leader, which is rarely the same as the leader of the original category.

Instead of understanding this concept of division, many corporate leaders hold the somewhat naïve belief that categories are combining. Synergy and its kissing cousin, strategic alliances, are boardroom buzzwords. Everything is converging.

Don't believe it. We no longer live in the world of mass marketing — it's dead. We are living in the world of mass customization. The story is this. It is a fact that around the world people are buying the same type of generic products — from cars to cosmetics, from fast food to fashion.

But within these broad categories is a fast-moving magnetic pull towards market fragmentation. Driven primarily by demographic and lifestyle changes, the endgame is category division. We now live in the world of mass customization. This is the Law of Division. Categories are dividing, not combining. Actually, people do want generic products, but they want them customized to suit their attitudes, opinions, lifestyles and personalities.

Japan's Yamaha Motor Co. Ltd. is another good example of the Law of Division. In 2002, the company unveiled a no-emission scooter for women. Few women like motorcycles, but scooters are less macho. Yamaha also found a segment of this market that comprised short-hop consumers who have strong concerns for the environment. So, the company launched The Passol, a model that is 40% lighter than the standard 50cc petrol-powered scooter, that moves with a quiet hum at 30 kilometers per hour. With a fully charged lithium-ion battery, it can travel 32 kilometers per hour.

According to Yamaha president Tooru Hasegawa, the sleek, small frame will catch the eye of space- and fashion-conscious consumers, and "make it easier for people who have never had an interest in motorcycles to enter into the two-wheeler world".

In Asia, if you want to go on holiday you can stay in a backpacker hotel, or a one-, two-, three-, four-, five- or, even, six-star hotel, not to mention a multitude of different resorts, also of varying descriptions. Raffles International, for example, offers top hotels such as the Raffles

Hotel for people who love tradition and heritage, and similar standard-service luxury hotels such as Raffles The Plaza in Singapore. To cater for the cosmopolitan business traveler, it has the Swissotel range. Like other hotel groups, it has a choice of rooms — economy, deluxe, extra and super deluxe, premium — and suites of all descriptions.

Consumer choice is usually driven by the utility value of the product or service offered, unless the brand is powerful enough to simplify their choice. In this situation, the decision tends to be influenced by what consumers want to do in those hotels with business colleagues, their families and friends, or on their own. But when you are outside the prestige part of the category, the truth is that the average consumer just does not know what they are buying! Category division confuses them unless this is clearly defined in the value proposition.

So the message here is: understand your market segment and, above all, when you create a division, don't confuse prospects.

⬿⬿

10

THE LAW OF THE HEART
(EMOTION)

Marketing strategies without emotion will not work.

It's a medical fact that emotion stimulates the mind 3000 times faster than rational thought. Why, then, do most Asian companies continue to rely on marketing strategies that appeal to the prospect's rational side?

Let's face it; it's an emotional world we live in. Many people say we live in a rational world but nothing could be further from the truth. The world is driven by emotion. Think of all your major life decisions — when you bought your first car; when you got your first date. Think about your first spouse (well, perhaps not). But that's the point — it's emotion that counts and emotion that drives our behavior.

Rational thought leads consumers to be interested but it is emotion that sells. This is why the leading companies in every industry build emotion into their marketing strategies. For instance, Kodak concentrates on capturing special moments, not just providing clear pictures.

Consumers use bi-cameral thought processes (left and right brain) when looking to buy. But the rational thoughts tend to be analytical and steer people away from emotional buy-in. It is the emotional thoughts that companies need to elicit from consumers, as shown in the examples below.

Rational	Emotional
Do I need it?	I want it!
What does it do?	It looks cool!
What does it cost?	I'm going to get it!
How does it compare to Brand X?	I only want this one!

If you concentrate on stressing rational features and attributes, this will stimulate rational questions in the prospect's mind. The shrewd marketers employ strategies that swing consumers to the right, making their decisions very emotionally driven and removing the questions that might drive the prospect elsewhere. The difference in the two approaches produces substantial and sustainable differences to the bottom line.

Asian companies have yet to learn the power of emotion in marketing, and all too often we see advertisements crammed with information about product features and attributes, rather than emotional benefits. In fact, consumers are often so confused with the array of features on, say, portable computers, laptops, etc, that they are at a loss as to what to buy.

The appeal of the Apple range cut through all the jargon with powerful emotional advertising. Steve Jobs once said in a press conference that people really aren't interested in terabytes and gigabytes: they want to know if they can have a pink one or a blue one — one that suits their personality. "Apple," Jobs says, "is not about bytes and boxes, it is about values." He has also said that some of the products Apple will be producing in the future will be so good you'll want to lick them. Perhaps that's going a bit far, but aesthetics does appeal to people's emotional drives. "Think Different" is Apple's tagline.

Omega's president, Stephen Urquhart, is spot-on when he says: "I think emotion is what drives people to a brand, but it is perhaps more short-lived today. People used to keep a watch for life...

you received a watch either at a religious ceremony or when you graduated. Or when you got married.

For a watch that's over S$100, technology is not why you buy it. You're buying it because of emotion, because of the brand, the design, what it's saying to you. Wearing it with feeling, so to speak. Nobody has a relationship with his or her toaster. But with a watch, there you're talking about emotion. You're talking about a relationship with the product."

TAG Heuer has been the most impressive market leader in sports watches in the world over the last few years; so successful that it has now been bought by the LVMH Group. TAG has positioned itself around the concept of inner strength; the fact that champions in all sports have to work just as hard, if not more, on the mental side of preparation and training as on the physical side. Ads which show an athlete hurdling over a giant razor blade, a gymnast high on a construction beam, a horse and rider jumping across from the top of one building to another, and Formula 1 drivers capture the viewer's emotions. Captions such as "Success is a Mind Game" and "What Are You Made Of?" reinforce the associations.

In the book business, Barnes & Noble Publishing Group president L. Alan Kahn says, "A lot of what is selling today is nostalgia."

Kodak says, "We don't need to yell from the top of the mountain. Our brand is relevant and attached to the emotional enjoyment that people get. Our consumers are using our product and connecting their emotions, experiences and memories."

Asian consumers are no different from anyone else in the world. We are all driven by emotion. Singapore Airlines (SIA) is in direct competition with some big players in a quest for international superiority and profitability. As we write, in a year of intense anxiety and recession for air travelers, SIA Group has just announced a six-month profit figure attributable to shareholders of S$774 million — an increase of 474 percent over the same period last year.

In air travel, apart from convenience, two things are of immense emotional importance to consumers — safety and service. Safety is a matter of security, track record, modern technology and maintenance. Service has a more personal flavor.

SIA set out to be a leader in service quality without compromising on safety, and its leadership in Asia has been based around the "Singapore Girl", symbolized by the female flight attendants. This emotional image has been sustained by meticulous attention to the detail of customer needs, individual grooming (including Pierre Balmain-designed service-attendant apparel) and the hint of Asian romantic appeal in advertising.

Even in this time of appalling travel fear, SIA moves forward and has spent over S$50 million on staff training. This is for a national airline in a country which has only four million people.

Carlos Ghosn, who has turned around the Nissan brand from huge debts in 1999 to half-year profits in 2002 of over US$2.5 billion, has achieved this by cutting costs and inefficiencies, but he has spent more on design and marketing. In explaining the real issue, he said that "Nissan forgot that the decision to buy a car has both irrational and emotional elements like design and status", and that the company "had previously focused only on technology and quality".

So don't always chase "share of wallet" — chase "share of heart" and the profits will come. Capturing minds is one thing; capturing hearts is quite another. But, remember; it is emotion that sells. Ignore the Law of the Heart at your peril.

11

THE LAW OF ATTRIBUTES

When you have to focus on attributes,
for every one of them, there is an opposite and
effective attribute.

In marketing, it is sometimes necessary to focus on product attributes. This is rational marketing (though, as Chapter 10, The Law of the Heart, has clearly shown, emotional marketing is better in most instances) and it is used either because you see the need to prove to consumers that you are up to date, or to demonstrate innovation.

What is more, if you can continuously innovate on products and their attributes, then you can own a leadership position as well. Sony is a good role model for attribute innovation and marketing. Through continuous innovation, it is managing to retain a global brand position by focusing on the rational side of consumers' buying behavior.

Sony is a leader brand. But all too often challenger brands attempt to emulate the leader.

"They must know what works," goes the rationale, "so let's do something similar." This is not good thinking. In the motorcycle market segment, everyone follows Honda's marketing strategies. Even their ads are similar. Honda is the clear market leader, and by following Honda in marketing communications, the competitors are reinforcing their position as followers. Consequently, Honda will continue to be market leader until the other competitors do something different.

It's much better to search for an opposite attribute that will allow you to play off against the leader. The key word here is "opposite" — "similar" won't do.

Marketing is a battle of ideas. So if you are to succeed, you must have an idea or attribute of your own to focus your efforts around. Without one, you had better have a low price. A very low price. The trouble is that leadership in operational costs of production that allow for low prices is very difficult to gain and sustain. Fighting on price is a death strategy; so avoid it wherever possible.

Some say all attributes are not created equal. Some attributes are more important to consumers than others. You must try and own the most important attribute. It becomes very difficult for your competitors if you gain the high ground.

An interesting scenario is if you can make the attribute itself into a brand. Rarely done, it has been accomplished in Asia by Cerebos Pacific Ltd, which owns Brand's. Brand's is a leading brand in the health-supplement category in many of its key markets such as Singapore, Thailand, Taiwan, China, Hong Kong and Malaysia. The Brand's product range includes a famous brand in itself — Brand's Essence of Chicken. The product, over 100 years old, has been trusted by generations for its healthy properties. (There used to be an Essence of Beef as well, but Asian tastes have made chicken almost a staple meal product, and beef was discontinued a long time ago.)

The product has a mystique about it that conjures up associations of health and vitality for the whole family. Cerebos has also made Brand's modern, introducing a caplet form, as well as the traditional liquid in the familiar green-and-yellow-labeled bottle. Brand's owns the "chicken and health" attribute and no other competitor is likely to be able to take that away.

Whilst on the subject of food and nourishment,

if you make a trip to any branch of McDonald's in Asia, you'll quickly see that McDonald's owns the attribute of "kids". Kids drag their parents to McDonald's all the time, which makes it very difficult for A&W and Burger King to compete for that section of the market.

In Singapore, for example, McDonald's has around 48% market share of the fast-food market, with Burger King about 20%. A&W is reduced to 2%. (The rest of this category is taken up with the KFC-Pizza Hut-Taco Bell chain at around 25% and Mos Burger at around 5%.)

If competitors can't beat McDonald's, they have to sacrifice this attribute. The other chains have to find another attribute that appeals to the rest of the market, and that's tough.

If you have to rely on attributes, you must own the best one; otherwise it's a constant challenge for market acceptance. Some smart companies turn their attributes into brand personality characteristics and concentrate on these in their marketing communications.

Land Rover is a good example of this. Worldwide, through videos and training, the company showed its sales staff how to take the rational attributes of the product and express them as emotional personality characteristics. So when market research revealed that Land Rover was seen as "robust", sales people were told to relate the product to consumers in terms of the characteristic of "guts and determination". Instead of 4x4 capability and engineering, the company talked about supremacy and leadership. The quirkiness of "individualistic" was changed to "individualism", and authenticity came to the fore instead of "heritage" with its museum-like, musty connotation. Land Rover taught its staff that they weren't selling vehicles; they were selling adventure and freedom. These characteristics were felt to be much more powerful and expressive of the Land Rover marque, and differentiated Land Rover products from the rest of the crowd.

Attributes are important in marketing, but they are easily copied. If you can't own the best one, you have to gain the high ground via another route.

❦❦

12

THE LAW OF CANDOR

When you admit a negative, the prospect will give you a positive.

It goes against corporate and human nature to admit a problem or a fault. For years, the power of positive thinking has been drummed into us. "Think positive" has been the subject of endless books and articles, and motivational speakers pass through Asian countries (charging huge fees) with a frightening intensity.

Positive thinking has been highly overrated. The explosive growth of communications in our society has made people defensive and cautious about companies trying to sell them anything. Admitting a problem is something that very few companies do. So it may come as a surprise to you that one of the most effective ways to get into a prospect's mind is to first admit a negative and then turn it into a positive.

First and foremost, candor is very disarming. Every negative statement you make about yourself is instantly accepted as the truth. Positive statements, on the other hand, are looked at as dubious at best. This is especially so with an advertisement. For example, in *The Sunday Times*, Singapore (20th October, 2002), an extremely large advertisement proclaimed:

"No.1 Worldwide

Ford Focus, best-selling car in the world in 2001."

Now even though a source reference is given in the ad (in this case Wheels Asia), the claim immediately starts people thinking about whether it is true. And if it is, why do they fail to see Ford Focus cars everywhere they go. Well, it may be a new model, but here we are heading towards 2003, so maybe not. By contrast, in the same newspaper there was another motoring ad:

"The NEW 2003 Corolla. Now in our showroom."

The second ad is less arrogant, and certainly invokes curiosity, as opposed to animosity.

You have to prove a positive statement to the prospect's satisfaction. No proof is needed for a negative statement. When a company starts a message by admitting a problem, people tend, almost instinctively, to open their minds. Think about the times that someone came to you with a problem and how quickly you got involved and wanted to help. Now think about people starting off a conversation about some wonderful things they are doing. You were probably a lot less interested.

With that in mind, you're now in a position to drive in the positive, which is your selling idea.

"Avis is only #2 in rent-a-cars" is a famous example. Not only was this an honest statement, which few companies appear to give these days, it was quite a shrewd marketing move. First of all, it led to the slogan "We try harder", which became a self-fulfilling prophecy amongst staff. Secondly, it put National Car Rental — the #3 — in a tricky spot. No company wants to publicly admit it is third.

So why go with the obvious? Marketing is often a search for the obvious. Since it is difficult to change a mind once it's made up, your marketing efforts have to be devoted to using ideas and concepts already installed in the brain. No program did this as brilliantly as the Avis program.

People sometimes complain about cooking smells in shopping malls from stalls cooking products on the premises. Famous Amos, the food chain, has around its outlets the words "free smells". Not only is this amusing and highlights a positive selling point in a friendly way (as the smells are pleasant to some people), it tells them that they can look at the products and won't get pestered to buy. And they don't. Guinness Stout was candid about one of its selling weaknesses. When a customer orders a draft Guinness, it takes a long time to pour, settle, and be topped up. It takes so long if it's done properly, that friends ordering regular beer are halfway to finishing drinking theirs by the time it's ready. Guinness, famous for its creativity in advertisements, turned this weakness into a strength by showing a customer patiently waiting whilst others watched, and then really enjoying the drink. The campaign slogan went something like, "If you can wait. Guinness."

One final note: The Law of Candor must be used carefully and with great skill. First, your "negative" must be widely perceived as a negative. It has to trigger an instant agreement with your prospect's mind. If the negative doesn't register quickly, your prospect will be confused and will wonder, "What's this all about?"

Next, you have to shift quickly to the positive. The purpose of candor isn't to apologize. The purpose of candor is to set up a benefit that will convince your prospect.

This law only proves the old maxim: Honesty is the best policy.

13

THE LAW OF SACRIFICE

You have to give something up in order to get something.

The Law of Sacrifice is the opposite of the Law of Extension (see Chapter 7). If you want to be successful in this fast-changing world, you have to be prepared to give something up.

There are three things to consider in this regard: product line, target market and constant change.

First, the product line. Where is it written that the more you have to sell, the more you sell?

The full line can be a luxury for a loser. If you want to be successful, you have to be very careful not to overextend it. For instance, Philip Morris' one Marlboro brand sells more than all the 200-plus cigarette brands held by British American Tobacco.

Marketing is a game of mental warfare. It's a battle of perceptions, not products or services.

And strong positive perceptions bring profits and asset value. For example, in the mind of the prospect, Marlboro owns the position that represents a personality of strength and independence. In the ads — which are reduced under lobby pressure — Marlboro country is wide open plains and big mountains; the cowboy (now in limited circulation as a not-so-desirable role model for youth) is always looking strong and independent; the red and white packaging is the same; even the horses look strong and independent. Cigarettes are under huge pressure from law suits now as viable brands for the future, but according to the Bangkok newspaper *The Nation* of 6th November, 2002, Marlboro is still the ninth-most valuable brand in the world at US$24.1 billion.

As we write, Coca-Cola Co. is in danger of losing more and more of its global value. It is pursuing relentlessly an aggressive "Think Local, Act Local" product strategy to reach more and more market segments with more and more products, so diluting the core brand position. And in 2001, we understand, Sony launched more than 10,000 products. It's hard to find the marketing resources to back all of those adequately. As we've said before, more can be less and less can mean more.

With the emphasis on product and not marketing, this mentality can be extremely damaging to the business. When Sony joined up with Ericsson, the Sony Ericsson president, Katsumi Ihara, said that a big investment in the new brand wasn't necessary because the name speaks for itself. "It doesn't make sense," he said, "to spend a lot of money — people will already know what it is. Instead of spending a lot of money on the brand, it makes more business sense to spend on the product." What we have seen since the launch, and with the introduction of new products, is the new business going nowhere, and Ericsson desperate for revenue and capital investment.

The target market is also important. The generalist tends to be weak, and the specialist strong. You can't be everything to everyone. Victoria's Secret is so successful because it concentrates on sexy underwear. By so doing, the brand has denied itself other opportunities, but they don't need them now. In fact, they are staying true to the Law of Focus (see Chapter 6). Ryan Air has taken market share and made big money with its basic air travel proposition for people with little spending power or an inclination to spend as little as possible. Air Asia is making inroads into the Malaysian market by offering similar value. Low prices and no pampering has its audience. In marketing there will always be people who look for value for money.

But you can't adopt this strategy when you are already in the premium price bracket. Lexus is losing in the image competition as it moves further down the consumer's disposable-income chain, offering products that are no longer outstanding. Consumers may as well buy the same product under a different name — Toyota — for a lower price. In Asia, Lexus has made little impact on the power brands of Mercedes and BMW. The opposite is also true. If Ryan Air were to change its strategy and try to compete with more luxurious travel, adding more frills, it would follow the route People Express chose some years ago. That company ended up avoiding bankruptcy by selling itself to Texas Air, which did it for them.

Honda is the undisputed king of the motorcycle category in Asia. But Honda's motorcycle identity has hurt them in automobiles. For example, while Honda is either first or second in the U.S. market in Japanese imported cars, the brand is a distant third in the Japanese market, which thinks of Honda as a motorcycle.

Finally, the third sacrifice: constant change. Where is it written that you have to change your strategy every year at budget review time?

If you try to follow the twists and turns of the market, you are bound to end up off the road. In fact, for many Asian companies, the biggest challenge is trying to catch up with the West.

Liu Chuanzhi, chairman of Legend Holdings — China and Asia's biggest manufacturer of personal computers — said, "The biggest challenge is that the industry changes so much." With 30% market share in China at present, Legend's market share limit at home will be achieved by 2005. Then the biggest challenge will be whether it can build an international brand or be a global OEM player and distribute for others. Whilst it knows the China market, it doesn't have enough knowledge of foreign markets to build a strong brand as yet. The OEM route, plus extensions into related businesses in the home market (for example, mobile phones) may be the sacrifice it has to make unless it can gain knowledge power in an ever-changing industry.

India's IT consultancy Wipro may have a problem on the horizon. By the end of March 2003, it is expected to achieve software exports of US$200 million. Companies like Nokia, Compaq and Home Depot use its services, and it has just landed a big contract with Sony to write IT applications. Wipro may gain rapid growth at the expense of becoming vulnerable to demanding clients like Sony that are looking for low-cost companies to design total business processes; in essence becoming outsourced arms of their businesses.

For those with established brand names already, the best way to maintain a consistent position is not to change in the first place. In order to stick to its basic positioning of authenticity in jeans, Levi's has realized, after one or two mistakes, that following the vagaries of fashion is sometimes not such a good idea. Maintaining its classic status — a positioning that transcends fashion — has been essential to the survival of the brand. Now it has created a portfolio of different brand names to take advantage of new market trends. Some have been successful, like Dockers. When your brand stands for something significant in people's minds, don't think you can move anywhere, anytime, anyplace.

Good things come to those who sacrifice.

14

THE LAW OF SUCCESS

Success often leads to arrogance, and arrogance to failure.

Ego is the enemy of successful marketing. Objectivity is what's needed.

When people become successful, they tend to become less objective. They often substitute their own judgment for what the market wants.

For example, some companies ruthlessly pursue consumer awareness as a valuable marketing metric, not realizing that 100% market awareness very rarely results in a market share of more than 25%. Nor does it guarantee trust. A great deal of money is wasted on advertising to gain brand awareness, but if the consumer doesn't trust the brand, it's finished. One company gained a brand awareness of 84% but a trust rating of only 17%. The result was huge losses and a takeover.

Success is often the fatal element behind the

rash of brand and line extensions. When a brand is successful, companies usually assume the name is the primary reason for the success. So they promptly look for other products to stick the name on.

Actually, it's the opposite. The name does not make a brand famous (although a bad name might keep a brand from becoming famous). A brand becomes famous because it makes the right marketing moves. In other words, the steps it takes are in tune with the fundamental laws of marketing.

You get into the mind first. You narrow the focus. You pre-empt a powerful attribute.

Coca-Cola is extending its product range more and more. Its "Think Local, Act Local" strategy is unlikely to produce great results. In fact, as we write, the company's market capitalization and brand value is declining alarmingly. It is in great danger of losing its #1 position in the world's top ten brands. The more this strategy is put into action, the more the core brand values are likely to be eroded. Pressure on numbers and category changes give rise to great temptations via extensions.

Extensions away from the main brand name — Qoo, for example — can do well for Coca-Cola. Qoo is a fruit-flavored drink with added vitamins for kids that is taking Asia by storm. The non-carbonated category needs to leave out the Coke name. But Vanilla Coke? That will only dilute the Coke brand and may repeat failures of the past.

The Virgin Group also has an air of invincibility. Richard Branson has an unshakeable faith in the fact that his Virgin brand can go anywhere, anytime into any category. It can't, and it needs to look more closely at why some of its businesses have succeeded and why some have not. The latest failure in Asia, with the closure of Virgin Mobile, should lead to some powerful marketing introspection.

Sometimes success puffs up your ego to such an extent that you put the famous name on other products. The result? Early success and long-term failure. The more you identify with your brand or corporate name, the more likely you are to fall into the extension trap. "Pride comes before a fall" is a common saying and one which should be heeded.

Ego can be helpful, though. It can be an effective driving force in building a business. Branson built a great brand around his own personality of fun and irreverence. What hurts is injecting your ego into the marketing business. Brilliant marketers have the ability to think like consumers think. They put themselves in the shoes of their customers. They don't impose their own view of the world on the situation. They think from the "outside in" not the "inside out". The one thing that Hallmark realized was that it was not really in the business of selling greetings cards; it was really in the relationship business.

It didn't extend into everything it could on the basis of its success; it concentrated on those businesses that reinforced its success. It wanted to help people express their feelings and strengthen the most important relationships in their lives. So it marketed videos, cable TV, real estate and other relationship-building categories.

Keep in mind that the world is built on perceptions anyway, and the only thing that counts in marketing is the consumer's perception. Consumers have associations with brands that are hard to shift but relatively easy to build on. But success can easily make companies forget who made them successful — customers.

Another factor at play here is that the bigger the company, the more likely it is that the CEO or top management loses touch with the front lines. This might be the single most important factor limiting the growth of a corporation. All other factors favor size. Marketing is war, and the first principle of warfare is the principle of force. The larger army, the larger company, has the advantage.

But the larger company gives up some of that advantage if it cannot keep itself focused on the marketing battle that takes place in the mind of the consumer.

15

THE LAW OF FAILURE

Failure is to be expected and accepted.

Too many companies try to fix things rather than drop things. "Let's restructure to save the situation" is their way of thinking. A better way of life is to recognize failure early and cut your losses. IBM should have dropped copiers and Xerox should have dropped computers years before they finally realized their mistakes.

Oldsmobile has at last been given its orders to go to the final parking lot. The management at General Motors failed to read the signs that had been flashing for years, and did not drop the brand. Attempts at repositioning using logo changes, product variations and so on did not remedy the situation, even though the company spent US$4 billion in the process.

Sometimes, it's the pressure to get the numbers

for sales and market share that causes people to take risks or ignore the obvious. In the fast-food war in Singapore, McDonald's tried to fix its competitive problem by co-branding with Hello Kitty! but lost credibility instead. The little cat promotional items were so much in demand that people were queuing for two blocks. Fighting broke out as people tried to jump the queues. One person bought more than 100 Big Macs, took the same number of cats, and promptly threw the burgers in the waste bin. Stocks ran out, and altogether it caused a massive dent in the McDonald's image.

Sometimes it's the culture of the organization that encourages people not to make or admit to mistakes. Many of you have probably worked in this type of company; where you get kicked or fired if you make a mistake, but nothing is said if you do things right! This is not a good culture. People tend to learn a lot from mistakes, but punishing staff for making mistakes doesn't mean that they won't make mistakes in future. It simply means that the mistakes will be covered up wherever possible.

This type of culture can lead to a conflict between the personal and the corporate agenda. Senior executives with high salaries and a short time to retirement are unlikely to make bold moves. Even junior executives often make "safe" decisions so as not to disrupt their progress up the corporate ladder. Nobody has ever been fired for a bold move they didn't make.

And this can lead to a failure to take risks. (It's hard to be first in a new category without sticking your neck out.) So in many Asian companies nothing gets done unless it benefits the personal agenda of someone in top management. This severely limits the potential marketing moves a company can make. An idea gets rejected not because it isn't fundamentally sound but because no one in top management will benefit personally from its success.

The Japanese are a bit different, as they tend to make consensus ideas. Thus, admitting to mistakes does not lead to an apportioning of blame to individuals. This "ego-less" approach is a major factor in making the Japanese relentless marketers. It's not that they don't make mistakes; but when they do, they admit them, fix them, and keep on going.

What if Asia had more companies like Intel and 3M?

3M uses the "champion" approach to publicly identify the person who will benefit from the success of a new product or venture. The hugely successful Post-it Notes took almost a dozen years to bring to market and Art Fry got the credit as the scientist who championed the product. The company's staff are also given a percentage of their working time to spend thinking about new products and experimenting. They can take time off their normal duties to play around with new ideas, some of which may just result in revolutionary products like Post-it. 3M knows that many ideas will be worthless but still gives employees the freedom to make mistakes. Failure is regarded as part of the success formula.

Intel even has risk-taking as a corporate value. This value is defined by behaviors, and there is a 360-degree assessment survey. Employees are given training kits that include team and individual exercises, written and video interviews with role models chosen from amongst the workforce, advice on concerns such as the nature of risks that could be taken without damaging quality, a list of resources, and so on.

The company searches for model employees who live the brand values, such as risk-taking, for its role-model advocate awards. Each year, nominations for this award are accepted, but the selection process is rigorous, with only three or four awards given out. Winners not only have to demonstrate that they are role models for all Intel's brand values, including risk-taking, but must also be outspoken advocates of them. Intel also recognizes and rewards such performers in monetary ways.

The point is that everyone makes mistakes, but you have to help them to learn from them, and reward them when they come up with great ideas. Failure can thus be turned into success.

❧❧

16

THE LAW OF
UNPREDICTABILITY

Unless you write your competitors' plans, you can't predict the future.

Implicit in most marketing plans is an assumption about the future. Yet marketing plans based on what will happen in the future are usually wrong.

With hundreds of computers, satellites in orbit, and an army of meteorologists, no one can predict with total accuracy the weather three days from now. So how do you expect to predict your market three years in advance?

There are those who would say that Asia's big problem is the lack of the long-term view; that Asian management is too short-term in its thinking. These concerns are real. But it's important to understand that short-term financial thinking drives many of Asia's marketing problems.

Most companies have an obsession with short-term profitability. And often companies that live by the numbers die by the numbers. Sometimes this applies in family-owned companies, where they want to hang on to as much money as they can and don't really understand the benefits that investment in branding and marketing can bring. These benefits are more intangible than factories and machines, where you can see something producing tangible outputs.

Sometimes it's complacency — "We're doing okay now, so why change?" There are lamentably few heads of companies who, like Peter Brabeck of Nestlé, can say: "We are not driven by quarterly profits...short-term performance is important, but we have to balance it against the long-term development of the company."

Good short-term planning means coming up with an angle or word that differentiates your product or company. Then you set up a coherent long-term marketing direction that builds a program to maximize that idea or angle. It's not a long-term plan; it's a long-term direction.

Sometimes complacency and the inability of the giants to move quickly can work in favor of smaller, nimble Asian companies. This happened in the Philippines when Colgate was outmaneuvered by a small brand called Hapee.

Typically, Asian companies often work for the big companies such as Unilever and Procter & Gamble. It's the old Original Equipment Manufacturing (OEM) business, where margins are thin, volumes are high, and the small company is very vulnerable to contract-switching by the big companies who give out the contracts. One of our clients had 80% of his business locked up in OEM work, and one company for whom he produced products cancelled a US$3 million contract overnight. Then he hadn't much of a business left.

Cecilio Pedro in the Philippines was in this kind of position, providing aluminum toothpaste tubes for Colgate. When Colgate switched to plastic tubes, Pedro was left in the lurch with a large pile of unwanted tubes.

He thought hard and did his own market segmentation, thinking about what adults and children wanted. For the children's market he filled his tubes with five different flavor toothpastes — melon, strawberry, orange, green apple and tutti-frutti. Kids would have nothing else after experiencing these and, within three years, the Hapee brand went from 1% to 20% of the market (in a country with a population of around 85 million). It took Colgate three years to come up with its own flavored toothpastes for the kids' segment.

Now Hapee has plastic tubes and co-brands with "Sesame Street" in response to Colgate's marketing attacks via campaigns with Barbie and Pokemon. Colgate is still the generic name for toothpaste in this country and has deep pockets when it comes to marketing spend, but Pedro's company, Lamoiyan, is doing very well, thank you.

One way to cope with an unpredictable world is to build an enormous amount of flexibility into your organization. As change comes sweeping through your category, you have to be willing to change, and change quickly, if you are to survive in the long term. Complex 10-year plans don't work. In fact, simpler three-year plans no longer work!

So what can you do? How can you cope best with the unpredictability? While you can't predict the future, you can get a handle on trends, which is a way to take advantage of change. One example of a trend is Asia's growing orientation towards good health.

For example, store sales of vitamins have rocketed up. Now stores selling just vitamin products abound. We know this is a trend and not just a fad (for the difference between the two, see Chapter 18, The Law of Acceleration), but how much can the market take? And companies cannot forecast the impact of external comment from "experts" in the field.

The latest comment to hit the news in Asia is that most of the Vitamin E products are actually of no benefit at all unless they contain Gamma Vitamin E. So the old Vitamin E is "killed" overnight and a new variant is in the limelight. Another set of heath products containing purely natural ingredients were selling very well as an anti-stress combatant until recently, when it was announced that research had linked one ingredient to severe side-effects, including cancer.

The danger in working with trends is extrapolation. Many companies jump to conclusions about how far a trend will go. If you believed the prognosticators of a few years ago, everyone today would be eating wholewheat salad sandwiches and steamed fish. Fried chicken and hamburger sales are doing just fine, by the way.

Equally dangerous is the common practice of assuming that the future will be a replay of the present. When you assume nothing will change, you are predicting the future just as surely as when you assume that something will change. Remember Murphy's Law? The unexpected will always happen. Whilst Nintendo and Sony are battling it out for the computer game platforms and products, they have taken their eye off the potential competition, and in November 2002 Nokia announced its entry into the huge market via its mobile technology.

While tracking trends can be a useful tool in dealing with the unpredictable future, traditional market research can sometimes be more of a hindrance than a help. Research is good at measuring the past. New ideas and concepts are very difficult to measure. No one has a frame of reference. People don't know what they will do until they face an actual decision.

Product life-cycles are shortening at an immense rate. With computers, it's now down to three or four months. So you have to innovate; but innovation requires an understanding of what consumers want next. Marketers have to work more closely with product developers, and product developers have to move faster.

More and more companies are now trying to

live with the consumer in an attempt to gain more insight into how consumers live their lives, what they want, how they feel and react to decisions and daily-life problems, etc. Think back to the famous reply made by Charles Revson, founder of Revlon Cosmetics, when asked what business Revlon was in: "We're not in the business of selling cosmetics," he said; "we're in the business of selling hope." Revson clearly saw that to think of his business as simply cosmetics would lead to non-differentiation. This real insight led to a great positioning and global success. It is significant that now Revson is no longer with the company, Revlon's results are regressing to the point of being dismal.

The latest attempt to revive the brand is to engage movie star Halle Berry as the Revlon "spokesperson" — an expensive endorsement, but it might bring hope back to the flagging brand.

In the never-ending search for insights that may bring a paradigm shift in thinking for brands and businesses, some companies are now hiring research crews to live for a few days with "prototype" consumers, in order to learn about how they think and behave in their everyday lives (bedroom and bathroom scenes usually excluded!). Traditional research — both quantitative and qualitative — has the drawback of relying on what consumers say, which is sometimes different from what they actually do in real life. You have to find out how to press the "hot buttons" that turn consumers on, and this really means gaining an understanding of what motivates them in real-life situations.

Companies trying to create consumer brands are waking up to the fact that the place to start understanding consumer behavior is in the home, where people live their real lives amidst all the emotions, relationships, family frictions, and relative untidiness, rather than in the office or a research room.

For example, Procter & Gamble has been filming housewives going about their daily routines, and noticed mothers multi-tasking. One mother was feeding her baby whilst cooking some food, and snatching glances at the television. In natural scenarios such as this, companies can see what programs and advertisements attract housewives, and what products they use and what products could be used.

A bank in the U.S. has also done this to discover the process of how families at various stages of their life-cycle discuss and make major financial decisions. For example, with home loans, what do people take into consideration besides interest rates when taking this major decision? What do they worry about and discuss, how do they decide which bank to go to, and who makes the decisions? Unilever in Malaysia has a policy of sending its marketing staff out into rural areas to live with villagers in underdeveloped areas to discover their ways of life and get closer to them, so they can help with brand relationships and product development.

One final point that's worth mentioning: there's a difference between "predicting" the future and "taking a chance" on the future. No one can predict the future with any degree of certainty; nor should marketing plans try. But the closer you can get to the consumer, the more likely you are to succeed.

≋≋

17

THE LAW OF HYPE

The situation is often the opposite of the way it appears in the press.

When things are going well, a company doesn't need the hype. When you need the hype, it usually means you're in trouble. Some reporters and editors tend to be more impressed by what they read in other publications than by what they gather themselves. Once the hype starts, it often continues.

When Virgin Mobile, the joint venture between Singapore Telecoms and the Virgin Group, was launched it was fairly low key. Street promotions and the like showed a gentle but confident entry into the market. It was going to be Asia's newest and best mobile-phone operator. But when subscribers failed to come in, there was more and more hype. Newspaper ads accelerated, getting more risqué every week. As the hype reached its peak, the public found out that Virgin Mobile had only 20,000 subscribers and was in trouble. Despite denials, the company closed down shortly afterwards.

In the heavily touted "office of the future", everything was going to be integrated into one electronic box. The last time we looked, there were separate personal computers, separate laser printers, separate fax machines with separate telephone numbers, separate copy machines, and so on. The office of the future is aptly named — a concept that still remains very much in the future. As for virtual offices, try getting into the lift at lunchtime. Remember the dot.com hype? Half of Silicon Valley real estate is now going for rock-bottom rental. Remember Pacific Century Cyberworks? It changed its name to PCCW in an attempt to forget all the hype it produced at the time when red ink was a significant part of its business.

Such predictions violate the law of unpredictability. No one can predict the future, not even a sophisticated reporter from the *Asian Wall Street Journal*. The only revolutions you can predict are the ones you have already started.

Neither the facsimile machine nor the personal computer took off like a rocket. The personal computer was introduced in 1974. It took IBM six years to strike back with the PC. Even the PC didn't start to really boom until a year-and-a-half later.

From time to time, no-frills food makes the headlines. With each revival, it is reported that this remarkable development will revolutionize the packaged-goods industry. Brands will be out. People will read the labels and buy products on their merits rather than on the size of the brand's advertising budget. The no-frills manufacturers have never managed to take away market share from the leading brands. It's really hype.

Capturing the imagination of the public is not the same as revolutionizing a market. The concept of the videophone was introduced at the 1964 New York World's Fair. Well, we're still waiting for it to become an affordable reality.

And what about the continuous hype surrounding 3G mobile phones? The truth is that companies that originated the concepts and terminology still do not know what this means, and the consumer isn't going to know for a long time. And what's more, so much hype has been blasted at consumers about the promises of 3G and its "potential" benefits that people are beginning to disbelieve in those promises. That gives marketing big problems.

Not that there isn't a grain of truth in every over-hyped story but, for the most part, hype is hype. Real revolutions don't arrive at noon with marching bands and coverage on the evening news. Real revolutions arrive unannounced in the middle of the night and kind of sneak up on you.

The real truth is that there will only be incremental steps forward, accompanied by lots of hype. The really smart marketers will be those that make the incremental and innovative steps credible and demonstrable. Then consumers will believe the hype and buy.

We can't leave this subject in Asia without talk of sales and promotions. Sales signs are the epitome of hype. There are closing-down sales, anniversary sales, Christmas sales, Hari Raya sales, Chinese New Year sales, New Year sales, renovation sales, back-to-school sales, moving sales, Mother's Day, Father's Day and Children's Day sales. They are fast becoming a way of life in Asia. "No sale, no buy," say lots of consumers. The response from businesses is: "No sale, no survive." So into the promotion and commodity trap they all go.

(For more on the subject of sales, see Chapter 19, The Law of Perspective.)

18

THE LAW OF
ACCELERATION

Successful programs are not built on fads,
they're built on trends.

A fad is a wave in the ocean, and a trend is the tide. A fad gets a lot of hype and a trend gets very little.

Like a wave, a fad is very visible, but it goes up and down in a big hurry. Like the tide, a trend is almost invisible, but it's very powerful over the long term.

A fad is a short-term phenomenon that might be profitable, but a fad does not last long enough to do a company much good. Furthermore, a company often gears up as if a fad were a trend. As a result, the company is often stuck with a lot of staff, expensive manufacturing facilities, distribution networks and inventories.

A fashion, on the other hand, can be seen as a fad that repeats itself. Examples: mini-skirts for women and double-breasted suits for men; bell-bottom jeans and baggies.

When the fad disappears a company often goes into a deep financial shock. Atari is a case in point. Coleco Industries and its Cabbage Patch Kids is another. It all looked great after launch and the Cabbage Patch novelties were flooding stores in all sorts of product formats. Five years later, Coleco sought protection from creditors under Chapter 11 legislation. Hasbro acquired the brand, managed it more gently and with a long-term perspective and it's now doing reasonably well.

Here's the paradox. If you were faced with a rapidly growing business that displayed all the characteristics of a fad, the best thing to do would be to dampen the fad. By dampening the fad, you stretch the fad out and it becomes more like a trend.

You see this a lot in the toy business. Some owners of hot toys want to put their hot-toy name on everything. The result is that it becomes an enormous fad that is bound to collapse. When everyone has a Ninja Turtle or a Power Ranger, nobody wants one anymore. The point is that early success brings about greed, and the owners fan the fad rather than dampen it.

On the positive side, Barbie dolls are a trend. This could easily have gone the other way but when Barbie was first invented in the fifties, the doll was never merchandised heavily into other areas. As a result, the Barbie doll has become a long-term trend in the toy business. If a company dampens a fad and extends the brand life with disciplined brand management, there is every chance that the fad could become a trend like Barbie.

Another fad that turned into a trend is Hello Kitty. Sanrio Co. from Japan invented the little cat based on a cartoon character. It has a button nose, two black-dot eyes, six whiskers, and a ribbon or flower in her hair. Hello Kitty has no mouth, and this represents a major source of emotional association for buyers, as they can project many different feelings onto the little cat. The owner and the cat can be happy, thoughtful, sad, or share any other feelings they want to, together.

Hello Kitty has developed into an icon with global appeal, with over 15,000 items available in 2000 and many more now. In addition to the ubiquity of Hello Kitty in Asia, it is in dozens of stores in the U.S., South America and Europe. It is adored by girls and women of all ages, and thanks to Sanrio's tight grasp on management of the brand, it has produced enormous profits, even through times of recession. Like Barbie, it has gained immortality in the form of perpetual youth.

To make the quantum leap from fad to trend, you have to get into the mind of the consumer and allow your brand to grow, develop and mature with its target audience. This demands tremendous discipline, forgoing some of the short-term gains for long-term value, and investment in consumer insight. Remaining relevant to the prospects is the key. Hello Kitty has done this by appealing to the girls of 20 years ago, who are now mothers and have daughters, with products that are relevant (such as bed sheets).

Fads and trends are relevant to all businesses, not just toys. They are applicable even to entertainment. Many successful entertainers are the ones that control their appearances. They don't get overexposed, appearing all over the place. They don't wear out their welcome.

Elvis Presley was restricted in his appearances and recordings by his manager, Colonel Parker. As a result, every time the King of rock 'n roll made a live appearance it was an event of enormous impact. So it is with Jackie Chan. The master of Kung Fu and the irreverent hero of Asia also limits his films and appearances.

However, the Asian marketing world is becoming littered with fads and failures. One of the biggest question marks now hangs over Bubble Tea. In Asia, tea has been a traditional drink for thousands of years (as opposed to coffee, which is a relative newcomer). The Bubble Tea phenomenon (the name comes from the bubbles formed when the tea is shaken) swept through Singapore in 2001, but it was old news in Taiwan, where it originated.

The craze spread rapidly, spawning more than 70 franchises with a variety of names such as Cool Station, Quickly, Black Pearl, Milk Girl and Jolly Bean. At the height of the Bubble Tea fad some outlets managed to sell over 500 cups per day, but within a year the craze had faded and many players have had to close down.

By contrast, coffee outlets are most certainly a trend, and the leader — Starbucks — has managed the trend. This has provided Asian companies with the opportunity to ride with the trend in many countries. The big difference between the coffee and tea examples is that the Bubble Tea owners are selling a variation on the product, tea, whilst the coffee-outlet owners are selling more than the product; they are selling lifestyle and brand associations, such as sociability. Starbucks is now opening one outlet per day around the world.

In Taipei, Eddy Liu created the Barista brand of coffee house. Eddie had flown around the world and seen the interest in coffee outlets. He started one up in 1996. In March 1998, Starbucks came into the market, but Barista didn't go out of business. In fact, it opened more outlets. Now it has 33 and US$10 million sales. Eddie Liu reckons the Taiwan coffee market is now worth US$100 million a year and rising. Other players have also come in. Michael Li intends to increase his branded chain of IS (Italian Style) to 60 outlets next year.

Go to any major city in Asia and you'll find Starbucks and its clones. When you're selling personality rather than product, it'll be a trend not a fad. Coffee houses that sell style, prestige, personality and innovative product will last.

The real key to sustaining a fad and making it a trend is product innovation. The leaders will always innovate to keep consumers interested. When Starbucks comes out with a Caramel Macchiato, to stay with the trend you'd better produce something similar.

The bottom line is that, if you want a good bottom line, forget fads. And when they appear, try to control them. One way to maintain a long-term demand for your product is never to totally satisfy the demand. People love and desire authenticity and scarcity, because there are too many products that are similar. Sometimes, not being able to have something is better than being able to have it. (See also Chapter 8, The Law of Exclusivity and Superiority.)

The best, most profitable, thing to ride in marketing is a long-term trend. Anyone for coffee?

❧❧

19

THE LAW OF PERSPECTIVE

Marketing effects take place over an extended period of time.

Is alcohol a stimulant or a depressant?

If you visit the bars, restaurants, clubs and discotheques on a Friday night after the end of the week's work, you'd swear that alcohol was a stimulant. It's the same in Hong Kong, Singapore, Seoul, Kuala Lumpur, Tokyo, Bangkok and all the other Asian cities you can think of. The noise and laughter are strong evidence of alcohol's stimulating effect. Yet, in the early hours of the morning, when you see a few happy-hour customers staggering, collapsing and even fighting, you'd swear that alcohol is a depressant.

Chemically, alcohol is a strong depressant. But in the short term, by depressing a person's inhibitions, alcohol acts like a stimulant.

Many marketing activities exhibit the same

phenomenon. The long-term effects are often the exact opposite of the short-term effects.

Does having a "sale" increase a company's business or decrease it? Obviously, in the short term, it usually increases it. But there's more and more evidence to show that sales decrease business in the long term by educating consumers not to buy at normal prices.

Apart from the fact that you can buy something for less, what does a sale say to a prospective customer? It says that your normal prices are too high. When the sale is over, consumers tend to avoid a retail outlet with a "sale" reputation.

To maintain volume, outlets find they have to run almost continuous sales. It's by no means unusual these days to walk through shopping malls and find a dozen shops in a row with "sale" signs in their windows. But anniversary sales, holiday sales and other ingenious ways of offering cut-price merchandise often lead to closing-down sales!

The coupon weapon is another marketing technique that can have a boomerang effect. There is no evidence that issuing coupons generates long-term sales. And once you start, you find you need a quarterly dose of coupon issues to keep sales levels on an even keel. Issuing coupons can act like a drug. You continue to do it because the withdrawal symptoms are just too painful.

Any sort of discounting, such as sales and the issuing of coupons, tends to educate consumers to buy only when you offer them a special deal. So the margins become, and stay, slim and get even skinnier over time. It's a vicious circle; business anorexia.

What if a company never started discounting in this way in the first place? In the retail field, the big winners are the companies that practice "everyday low prices" — companies like Courts, Macro, Giant, Wal-Mart, Watson's, Carrefour, Tesco and warehouse outlets.

In many other areas of life (spending money, taking drugs, having sex), the long-term effects of your actions are often the opposite of the short-term effects. Why, then, is it so difficult to comprehend that beneficial marketing effects take place over an extended period of time?

Building a brand takes time. But brands bring premium prices. They get companies out of the commodity trap, whereas price discounting and other short-term sales boosters only dilute brand image. And image is everything in marketing if you want to avoid the death strategy — fighting on price.

An Armani outlet once held a sale. A huge banner was hung on the face of the building in a sophisticated Asian city, with the two words 'Armani' and 'Sale'. It would have been much better for the image of this luxury brand, and more effective in building relationships, not to dump stock in this way. Instead, it could have been turned into a brand-building opportunity by inviting (privately) all regular customers to an exclusive sale event in another location. By doing so, Armani's image would have been protected rather than cheapened, the company would have maintained exclusivity, and brand loyalty would probably have improved.

It looks easy, but marketing is not a game for amateurs.

❦

20

THE LAW OF
THE OPPOSITE

*If you're shooting for second place, your strategy
is determined by the leader.*

In strength there is weakness. Wherever the leader
is strong, there is an opportunity for a would-be
#2 to turn the tables. If you want to establish a
foothold on the second rung of the ladder, study
the company that's above you. Where and why is it
strong? Where are its weaknesses, and how can you
turn its strengths into weaknesses? Look at the focus
of the leader, but don't try to emulate it. Try instead
to be different.

When you look at consumers there are two kinds
in any given category. There are those that want to
buy from the leader and there are those that do
not. Your focus should be the latter. In other words,
by positioning yourself against the leader, by
appearing to be different, you take business away
from all the other alternatives to #1. Yet too many

brands tend to try to emulate the leader.

Let's take a look at some examples. The vodka market was turned upside down by Absolut. Throughout the history of spirits, heritage and provenance were all-important, and so whiskey, vodka and other spirits were marketed this way. In the case of vodka, Smirnoff and Stolichnaya sold Russian associations. Absolut took the opposite route, marketing its product more as a fashion statement than a spirits brand. Apparently, it is now in the top five best-selling liquor brands, and its average price is 20% higher than its competitors'.

Traditionally, ICI has been the leader in household paints, emphasizing colors, durability, smooth finish and quick-drying attributes. Nippon Paint has not tried to take on the ICI power brand by trying to offer better elements concerned with the same attributes. It has moved away from these and come up with products that provide and emphasize protection from bacteria. Sure, it has a good range of colors and so on but its positioning is built around its special formula which protects the living environment from many types of bacteria (such as MRSA, E-Coli and Staphylococcus Aureus) to prevent the spread of asthma, flu and dysentery.

Moving on to more palatable matters, reading enriches the mind and supposedly those people who read more complex material are the learned ones. There are many expert books on all subjects produced by the large publishing houses, but this is their weakness. They do not cater for the 99% of the reading population who want to know simply what a subject is all about. For example, the advent of the personal computer brought with it considerable confusion and a lack of knowledge about how to get the best out of their PCs, or how to get on the Internet and explore the world of Windows. The manuals were tedious and often written by experts who were out of touch with the normal person. Frustrated computer customers just wanted a simple guide to, say, the complicated DOS operating system.

So out came the "For Dummies" series, starting with "DOS For Dummies" in November 1991. Most bookstore chains did not want to carry the series as they felt audiences would be insulted. But let's face it, on most subjects most people are dummies. The rest is history, and to date the "Dummies" series has sold more than 100 million copies, showing you how to do everything — cook, garden, manage finances, run a business, eat well, have good sex etc. In only 10 years, For Dummies has become a fun and informative brand.

Who is the greatest British movie spy? Right first time — James Bond, the suave and dashing 007. The James Bond series is a goldmine and is in its 40th-anniversary year, an achievement unique in the movie industry. So how can you compete? By doing the opposite. The opposite is Austin Powers! If James Bond is suave and dashing, Austin Powers is crude and outrageously dressed. If James Bond is about subtle humor, Austin Powers is slapstick. But they do have two things in common — women find them irresistible and they both sell! The Law of the Opposite works in all categories.

Sometimes you have to be brutal. When Heineken had a massive market share of the U.S. imported-beer market, Kronenbourg, the French beer, tried to break in with taste-testing ads. Of course, when you do taste tests your product normally comes out top, and Kronenbourg advertised this advantage. Heineken's reply in its ads went something like this: "Kronenbourg; the reason the French drink wine."

But don't simply knock the competition. The Law of the Opposite is a two-edged sword. It requires homing in on a weakness that your prospect will quickly acknowledge. Then quickly twist the sword. When Beck's beer arrived in the United States it had a problem. It couldn't be the first imported beer (that was Heineken), nor could it be the first German beer (that was Lowenbrau). Recognizing this, Beck's repositioned Lowenbrau by saying: "You've tasted the German beer that's the most popular in America. Now taste the German beer that's the most popular in Germany." Beck's became the second-largest-selling European beer in America. Now Warsteiner is doing to Beck what Beck did to Lowenbrau. Warsteiner is advertising its brand as "The best-selling German beer in the world."

Marketing is often a battle for legitimacy. The first brand that captures the concept is often able to portray its competitors as illegitimate pretenders.

A good #2 can't afford to be timid. When you give up focusing on #1, you make yourself vulnerable, not only to the leader but to the rest of the pack.

21

THE LAW OF ORIGIN

Where brands come from is often more
important than how good they are.

In Asia, the origin of products and services is very important. As a generality, prospects think that if it's local, it's not so good. But if the brand is from another, more developed country, especially if it's a Western country, then it must be good.

The Law of Origin means that to be accepted in the marketplace, you have to have credibility. For many Asians, a Western bank is better than a local bank even when the products and service quality might be similar. A local soap is as good as a foreign soap in performance but, given the choice and spending power, people won't buy it. The country of origin makes the difference. It's back to perceptions again.

For many decades Asian countries have had a problem in getting people to believe that products originating from their region are of good quality. There's nothing wrong with the products — from most countries in Asia they are of world-class quality. But put "Made in China" on a product and it won't sell well abroad, because most people's minds are already firmly made up on this issue.

People just will not believe that quality can come from developing countries. What makes things worse is that even the locals think the same. Go to a supermarket in most Asian countries and you will find housewives pushing aside home-made produce and looking carefully to ensure there is a foreign brand name there. This explains why some Asian companies export and then re-import their brands.

It took the Japanese 30 years to change people's minds on the quality topic, and other countries are still trying. Now Japan has a record of great quality and has been successful at moving into many markets, including the U.S. In the United States 30 years ago, Japanese companies were seen as cheap copies of low quality. Now a Toyota Corolla attracts an 8% premium and generates four-times the volumes of the General Motors Prizm, even though the only difference is the marque or badge. They are even produced on the same factory line!

Names are a perceptual influence, and can turn people on or off. One of the most consistent and profitable brands in Asian retail clothing is Giordano. It sounds Italian, but it's a Hong Kong brand. Italy is famous for fashion and style, and the brand name reinforces the perception.

Bonia sells leather goods and other accessories that have style and quality and that sell at international luxury-goods prices. Bonia may sound Italian, and has that perception of being European, but it is a Malaysian brand.

Diamonds may be forever but not so company names. Incorporated in Singapore during November 1970, Lee Hwa Holdings became publicly listed on the Singapore Stock Exchange in May 1999. By 2001, however, the company's name had changed to Aspial Corporation Limited, which now owns both Aspial and Lee Hwa jewelry brands.

For chief executive Koh Wee Seng, the name "Lee Hwa Holdings" simply does not cut it in the international market, where he wants to be. "If we're really serious about launching Singapore's first international jewelry brand," he says, "a Western name is more appropriate, to suit the positioning of our brand in the global market." So out went

Lee Hwa Holdings, and in came Aspial Corporation Limited.

Product is important for a company setting its sights on the world's brand-conscious jewelry market. Successful brands have to generate the perception of difference and have great quality. So the company led the market in the minimalist white-gold jewelry and this is still a hot product range. In 2001, it set the jewelry scene alight with its 19-carat solid Purple Gold collection. Purple gold was not new but getting the metal to a stage where it could be incorporated in jewelry was. This development, created with Singapore Polytechnic, helped Aspial become a market leader.

Product development is based at the company's factory in Singapore, but Aspial's designs are developed by teams from Singapore, Germany and Italy to create international appeal. The products are now sold in Tokyo, Seoul, Taipei, Beijing, Dubai, Frankfurt and London. Aspial's goal is to achieve S$1 billion in revenue and have 500 outlets around the world within five years, either through concessionaires, franchisees, or its own shops.

Haier is another company that is playing the origin game well from a different angle. As a manufacturer of white goods, such as refrigerators, from China, it was hardly expecting a great reception in the U.S., despite its world-class quality. So building at low cost and exporting wasn't a real option.

Instead, Haier built a factory in Camden, South Carolina, and began marketing products with the label "Made in the U.S.A.". Also, rather than compete with companies like Whirlpool head-on, it went for niche markets, producing wine coolers and other innovative products. Its market share of the small-refrigerator market in the U.S. is 30%. Haier now has plants in 13 countries, sells its products in 160, and aims to be a global brand.

What Haier must be careful of is to avoid too many brand extensions, as it has now gone into TV sets, air-conditioners, mobile phones, PC peripherals and restaurants (see Chapter 7, The Law of Extension).

22

THE LAW OF RESOURCES

Without adequate funding and expertise an idea won't get off the ground, and a brand cannot be built.

If you have a good idea and you've picked up this book thinking that all you need is a little marketing help, this chapter will help straighten out your thinking.

Even the best idea in the world won't go very far without the money to get it off the ground. Inventors, entrepreneurs, and assorted idea-generators often think that all their good ideas need is professional marketing help.

Nothing could be further from the truth. Marketing is a game fought in the mind of the prospect. You need money to get into a mind. And you need money to stay in the mind once you get there.

You'll get further with a mediocre idea and a million dollars than with a great idea alone. And since the dot.com collapse, venture capitalists have become much harder to find, and more cautious when you find them.

Many entrepreneurs and managers think that advertising is the answer, but costs increase all the time. What's more, advertising hits mass audiences, many of which may not be interested in your idea at all. So a lot of money is wasted in TV commercials and print media.

Remember, on average, every person gets hit by between 1,500 to 3,000 "pitches" a day from companies wanting to sell them something. So intense is the competition. Bearing this in mind, direct marketing, Internet marketing and public relations can be much more cost-effective. But you have to know your target audience and your messages have to be relevant.

One of the major obstacles faced by marketers in Asia is the lack of support from top management. They still do not understand that brands are assets in their own right and need investment to make them grow. The knee-jerk response to intensive competition is to fight on price and promotional strategies that dilute brand image and encourage price wars. As a consequence there are few great Asian brands.

When we talk to CEOs, they are very happy to show us their latest billion-dollar building or factory, or million-dollar machine. But when we ask them about marketing spend, the percentage of sales tends to be extremely low. Marketing equates to sales in their minds, and they are number-driven in this respect. They are very reluctant to spend on marketing for the long term, and are obsessed with short-term profits. As a result, they often ignore the laws of marketing we have described in their desperate pursuit of quarterly, half-year or annual numbers. To many CEOs, marketing is largely intangible. They cannot feel it, touch it, or watch it producing things instantly. So they worry about payback.

Whilst large brand-conscious companies such as Unilever and Procter & Gamble from the U.K. and U.S.A. spend about 11–12% of sales on advertising and promotion, and around 20% or more on total marketing and brand-building activities annually, most Asian companies just shudder at the thought.

This mind-set is slowly changing as CEOs and financial institutions understand more about brands and the role of marketing in building brands. They see Western brands being valued in dollars-and-cents terms. They are beginning to realize that the worth of a brand can be multiples of the net assets of the company itself. The word is out that brands are being put on balance sheets, and that brand valuation is being used for a variety of strategic purposes. The payback on marketing can now be measured with a considerable degree of accuracy, and they can see the returns. Today's marketers now have other tools at their disposal that can measure intangible emotional associations such as trust and loyalty.

As damaging in Asia as the lack of marketing financial support is the lack of high-level marketing expertise. In Asia, two-thirds of the population is under 35 years old. Consequently, there are many young people who are promoted quickly into very senior positions without a great deal of experience. Training and professional learning are key needs, and we hope that this book will contribute in this regard.

All of this means that it is even more important that you abide by the laws of marketing. They are immutable, and if you use them you will not be disappointed. Follow these rules and you'll be on the fast track to success. You will rise above the competition, gaining clarity and focus.

And above all, you will help build the most valuable asset(s) your company will ever have — its brand(s). The key to successful marketing that sums up the 22 Laws is differentiation. If consumers don't perceive your brand(s) as being different from those offered by the competition, you won't win the marketing war. The battle for consumer minds is a battle of perceptions not products.

INDEX

Bestselling titles from
Jack Trout

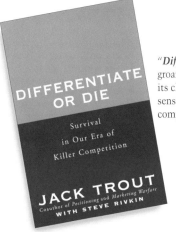